Indian Renaissance and Indian English Poetry

Indian Renaissance and Indian English Poetry

SUBHAS CHANDRA SAHA

PRESTIGE

Published by
Prestige Books
3/28, East Patel Nagar
New Delhi 110 008

ISBN: 81-7551-035-8

1998

Photo Typesetting by
Pivot Computers
Delhi 110 006
Ph. 2934490

Printed at
Chaman Offset Printers
New Delhi 110 002

Contents

Dedicated to

Professor Visvanath Chatterjee

Preface

There has been an on-going controversy about the existence of Indian English poetry: whether Indian English poetry has any merit as poetry, whether it can be considered a part of Indian literature, and whether it should exist at all! All these vexatious questions aroused my curiosity about the origin of this poetry. The book embodies my findings that the nineteenth-century English poetry of India is a by-product of the Indian renaissance that began in Bengal.

The first chapter records the main events that ushered in the Bengal Renaissance in the nineteenth century. It shows that the English poetry of Bengal was the product of historical forces operating there at that time. The Bengal Renaissance and the development of English poetry of Bengal during the nineteenth century occurred simultaneously and ran parallel to each other.

The second chapter chronicles the publications of poetry books in English by the Bengali poets in the nineteenth century. Since those publications have become rare, and some of them are not even available in India, I have traced the history of the nineteenth-century English poetry of Bengal with all the available factual details.

The third chapter highlights the main events of the Bengal Renaissance. It enumerates the four major characteristics of the Bengal Renaissance: (1) the influence of English education, (2) social reforms, (3) the rediscovery of the glorious past of India, and (4) intense nationalism and patriotism. These four major characteristics are reflected in the nineteenth-century English poetry of Bengal.

In the fourth chapter, the impact of English education on the nineteenth-century English poetry of Bengal as manifested in its assimilation of the influence of British poetry and its propagation of Christianity as a form of religion is discussed in detail with reference to the works of almost all the poets.

In the fifth chapter, the reformistic zeal that characterized the activities of the leaders of the Bengal Renaissance has been traced in the nineteenth-century English poetry of Bengal.

In the sixth chapter, the other characteristic of the Bengal Renaissance, namely, the re-discovery of the glorious past of India has been shown to be a major theme in the nineteenth-century English poetry of Bengal.

In the penultimate chapter, the last characteristic of the Bengal Renaissance, namely, intense nationalism and patriotism, has been shown as one of the chief characteristics of the nineteenth-century Indian-English poetry of the time.

In the last chapter, I have drawn the conclusion that the nineteenth-century English poetry of Bengal embodied the profound emotional and imaginative responses of the highly endowed Bengali poets who chose English as the medium of poetic expression during the nineteenth century, in the context of re-awakening and resurgent Bengal. Hence this poetry has not only an over-all social relevance but also a human significance and worth of universal quality.

Nineteenth-Century Bengal

After a long period of mental and intellectual lethargy and ennui as reflected in their economic, social and cultural history, the people of Bengal suddenly received a life-giving jolt from their contact with the English people and their culture by the end of the eighteenth century. Atul Chandra Gupta rightly points out: "the conquest and occupation of a large part of India by the English East India Company brought Bengal into contact with the civilization and culture of Europe, ancient and modern, and caused the Bengal Renaissance."[1]

After the advent of certain liberal and humanitarian British administrators like Warren Hastings, William Jones and Bentinck, and Christian missionaries like Carey and Duff who later earned the reputation of great orientalists and promoters of education and enlightenment among the natives of Bengal, the educated Bengalis, who went to study at recently established English schools and colleges to imbibe the liberal and progressive elements of Western education and culture, became keenly aware of the rapid progress achieved in every area of science and arts in England and other parts of Europe.

Rammohan Roy (1774-1833) is said to be "the inaugurator of the Modern Age in India."[2] In an appeal dated December 11, 1823 to Lord Amherst, the then Governor-General (1823-1828), Rammohan Roy wrote: "As the improvement of the native population is the object of the government, it will consequently promote a more liberal and enlightened system of instruction, embracing mathematics, natural philosophy, chemistry and anatomy, with other useful sciences which may be accomplished with the sum proposed by employing a few gentlemen of talents and learning educated in Europe, and providing a college furnished with the necessary books, instruments and other apparatus."[3] This conclusively demonstrates the eagerness and zeal with which the pioneers of the Bengal Renaissance welcomed the Western education and culture to rejuvenate the withering intellectual life of the Bengalis.

Henry Louis Vivian Derozio (1809-1831), another pre-eminent usherer of the Bengal Renaissance, addresses India as "My fallen country" in a sonnet entitled "To India—My Native Land."[4] In order to bring about a change in the condition of his native land, Derozio steeped himself in, and inspired his associates with, "the intoxicating freedom urge of the French Revolution and a passion for freedom of thought and liberation from the dead weight of all tradition."[5]

On March 7, 1835, Lord Bentinck resolved, on the advice of Thomas Babington Macaulay (1800-1859),[6] Chairman of the Committee of Public Instruction, that "the great object of the British Government ought to be the promotion of European literature and sciences among the natives of India, and that all funds appropriated for the purpose of education would be best employed on English education alone."[7]

The intention and goal of the reformers and leaders of the Bengal Renaissance, like Rammohan Roy and Derozio, were to infuse the spirit of progress and modernity into the life of Bengalis through the medium of English education and Western culture. The intentions of the administrators were, however, mixed. Though they conceded the demand of the enlightened Bengali intellectuals in favour of English education as opposed to the demand of the "Orientalists" who advocated the propagation of Sanskrit, they seized the opportunity to utilize the zeal of the "Anglicists" to create a climate of reception for the language and literature of their country, and thus establish their rule and administration in India through a set-up of bureaucrats and aristocrats nurtured on the English language and culture.

John B. Alphonso-Karkala observes: "The intention of providing English education was not to educate the masses of India but only a segment of the middle class."[8] In continuation, he comments: "To strengthen Bentinck's policy, Lord Hardinge, the Governor-General (1844-48), virtually made English education the only passport to higher appointments available to the Indians in the Company's various services."

After the educational policy in favour of English was formulated, and implemented through corresponding systems in Bengal throughout the nineteenth century, the educated Bengalis developed habits and outlook that reflected their English educational background. They started using the English language not only in their official and public life but also for their private day-to-day purposes. They became so enamoured of English that as Michael Madhusudan Dutt is said to have hinted, they even dreamt in English. Their obsessive fascination with English emboldened them to express their inmost feelings in the foreign language, acclimatizing it to the local situations and mores, as far as possible, making it a vehicle for the embodiment of their sensibility and imagination. Thus they created a new form and style of poetry—the English poetry by Bengalis. The first poet in this new form and style turned out to be a Eurasian, H.L.V. Derozio.

The adoption of English for the composition of poems by the educated and Westernized Bengalis is a corollary of the forces of history operating in the nineteenth-century Bengal. M.K. Naik remarks: "Indian English literature began as an interesting by-product of an eventful encounter in the late eighteenth century between a vigorous and enterprising Britain and a stagnant and chaotic India."[9] The successive Bengali poets, writing their poetry in English after Derozio, created a body of literature that was expressive of the several movements going on in the nineteenth-century Bengal. The reforms advocated and propagated by Rammohan Roy and Derozio in the early decades of the nineteenth century initiated a chain of events that entirely transformed the social and cultural perspective of the province, and later, of the whole country. In this context R.C. Majumdar observes: "Bengal passed in course of a single century from the Medieval to the Modern Age."[10] He quotes from Sir Jadunath Sarkar in support of his effort to characterise the nineteenth-century in Bengal as the period of the Bengal Renaissance: "it was truly a Renaissance, wider, deeper, and more revolutionary than that of Europe after the fall of Constantinople."

The reforms undertaken by Rammohan Roy and Derozio in the intellectual and religious spheres, the innovations introduced in Bengali poetry and drama by Michael Madhusudan Dutt, the spectacular flowering of the art of fiction in the novels of Bakimchandra Chatterjee (1838-1894), the exemplary activities of the Christian missionaries and Bengali educationists like Vidyasagar (1820-1891) in the area of education, the re-discovery of the glorious past of India by the Orientalists, and the religious and spiritual re-orientation brought about by the great sages of Bengal like Debendranath Tagore (1817-1905), Keshab Chandra Sen (1838-1884), Ramakrishna Paramhanso (1835-1885) and Swami Vivekananda (1863-1902), present a splendid spectrum of events and achievements that created an unprecedented stir in the psychological and intellectual life of the nineteenth-century Bengalis. This led to an inevitable revolution in the domain of art and culture of Bengal. Nineteenth-century English poetry of Bengal is a literary outcome of this revolution. According to M.K. Naik, "The rise of Indian English literature was an impact of this Indian renaissance."

This renaissance was not confined to the town of Calcutta, the new capital of British India, or to the province of Bengal; it spread to the other parts of the country and finally caused "Indian Awakening." Sir Jadunath Sarkar sums up the situation: "If Periclean Athens was the school of Hellas, the eye of Greece, mother of arts and eloquence, that was Bengal to the rest of India under British rule."[11] He further analyses the situation: "In this new Bengal originated every good and great thing of the modern world that passed on to the other provinces of India. New literary forms, reform of the language, social reconstruction, political aspirations, religious movements and even changes in manners that originated in Bengal, passed like ripples from a central eddy, across provincial barriers to the farthest corners of India." (II, 498)

English poetry of Bengal is one "good and great thing" of Bengal, and it may be designated one of the "new literary forms" that continues to be used with increasing improvements by poets in the rest of the country in successive years and contributes to the formation of Indian English literature. In this book, I would focus critical attention on the initial stages of development of Indian English poetry that originated in Bengal out of a revolutionary upheaval that shook India out of her prolonged hibernation.

Though English poetry of Bengal may owe its origin to English language and education, it reflects, both thematically and stylistically, the zeitgeist of the nineteenth-century Bengal. All the major characteristics of the Bengal Renaissance are mirrored in the poetry of H.L.V. Derozio, Kasiprasad Ghosh, Soshee Chunder Dutt, Madhusudan Dutt, Govin Chunder Dutt, Hur Chunder Dutt, Greece Chunder Dutt, Toru Dutt, Swami Vivekananda, Manmohan Ghose and Aurobindo Ghose.

In the next chapter I will present a broad sketch of the history of poetry written originally in English by Bengalis during the nineteenth century. In the third chapter I will survey the major events of the Bengal Renaissance, and finally enumerate its predominant characteristics. In the later chapters I will engage myself in a critical analysis of the nineteenth-century English poetry of Bengal in order to find out and trace how far this poetry embodies the characteristics of the Bengal Renaissance that nourished and developed it.

NOTES

1. Atul Chandra Gupta, ed., *Studies in the Bengal Renaissance* (Calcutta,1958), Introduction, p. xi.
2. Nemai Sadhan Bose, *Indian Awakening and Bengal* (Calcutta, 1976), p. 31.
3. Raja Rammohan Roy, "Letter on English Education, dt. December 11, 1823", *The English Works of Raja Rammohan Roy* (Allahabad, 1906), pp. 271-74.

4. H.L.V. Derozio, *Poems* (Calcutta, 1980), p. 2.
5. Sushoban Sarkar, *On the Bengal Renaissance* (Calcutta, 1979), p. 26.
6. T.B. Macaulay, "Indian Education Minute," *Prose and Poems*, selected by G.M. Young (Cambridge, Mass., 1952), pp. 719-30.
7. Henry Sharp, *Selections from Educational Records* (Calcutta, 1920), Vol. I, p. 130.
8. John B. Alphonso-Karkala, *Indo-English Literature in the Nineteenth Century* (Mysore, 1970), p. 11.
9. M.K. Naik, *A History of Indian English Literature* (New Delhi, 1982), p. 1.
10. R.C. Majumdar, *Glimpses of Bengal in the Nineteenth Century* (Calcutta, 1960), p. 21.
11. J.N. Sarkar, *History of Bengal* (Dacca), Vol. II, p. 498.

The Nineteenth-Century English Poetry of Bengal

The beginning of English poetry of Bengal might have been sudden, but it clearly shows a definite line of development. The first book in the field is H.L.V. Derozio's *Poems*, printed for the author in 1827 by Baptist Mission Press, Calcutta. In 1828 Derozio brought out another volume of poems under the title *The Fakeer of Jungheera, a Metrical Tale, and Other Poems*, printed by Samuel Smith & Co., Hur-Karu Library, Calcutta.

Before he published the books, Derozio had been contributing poems to *India Gazette*, edited by John Grant, under the pseudonyms "Juvenis," "Henry," "East Indian," etc.[1] The first magazine publication of his poems is found in *India Gazette* dated 22 January 1824. His poems were also printed in the *Calcutta Magazine*, the *Indian Magazine*, the *Bengal Annual* and the *Kaleidoscope*.[2] Besides these, C. Paul Verghese mentions two other magazines, *The Bengal Journal* and the *Calcutta Literary Gazette* which printed Derozio's poems.[3]

In 1907 there came out *The Poetical Works of Henry Louis Vivian Derozio*, edited by B.B. Shah, with a brief memoir of the author by E.W. Madge, published by Sento & Co., Calcutta.

In 1923 there appeared a larger volume entitled *Poems of Henry Louis Vivian Derozio: A Forgotten Anglo-Indian Poet*, with an Introduction by F.B. Bradley-Birt, published by Oxford University Press, Oxford. This is the last definitive edition of Derozio's poems, reprinted by Oxford University Press, Calcutta in 1980.

Still many more poems by Derozio lie scattered in several contemporary journals, which are not yet collected in book form, as is evident from the excerpts quoted by Pallav Sengupta in his book already referred to.

Derozio is born of a Portuguese father and an English mother. He is called Eurasian by some of his biographers. Nevertheless, R.K. Dasgupta unequivocally calls him a Bengali poet: Derozio is not one of the Poets of John Company; he is a Bengali poet who wrote his poems in English."[4] But in 1921 T.D. Dunn included Derozio's poem "On the Abolition of Suttee" in his *Poets of John Company*, intended to be a

"Collection of Verse Written in India by Englishmen," though he excluded Derozio's poems from his other book titled *A Bengali Book of English Verse* (1918). Dasgupta's standpoint is, however, corroborated by the opinion of recent Bengali scholars on Derozio like Benoy Ghose,[5] Jogesh Chandra Bagal,[6] R.C. Majumdar,[7] Susobhan Sarkar[8] and Pallav Sengupta.[9] Derozio undoubtedly is the foremost pioneer of English poetry of Bengal, just as Raja Rammohan Roy is the inaugurator of Modern Age in Bengal.

The next Bengali poet to publish poems in English is Kasiprasad Ghose (1809-1873). His collected poems were published under the title *The Shair, or Minstrel and Other Poems* by Scott and Co., Calcutta in 1830. The book was dedicated to Governor-General Lord William Bentinck. His other book is titled *The Hindu Festivals* which, however, never saw the light of day. The poems were published in the *Calcutta Literary Gazette*.[9]

Whatever may be the literary merit of Kasiprasad Ghose's poems, his book evoked favourable and encouraging responses from several Englishmen of both India and England. D.L. Richardson, a teacher at the Hindu College, wrote appreciatively of his verse in the *Literary Gazette, Calcutta,* dated November 1834: "Let some of these narrow-minded persons who are in the habit of looking down on the natives of India with arrogant and vulgar contempt read this little poem ("Boatmen's Song to Ganga") and ask themselves—could they write better verses not in a foreign tongue but their own?" Theodore Dunn found Kasiprasad Ghose's verses "agreeably imitative and everywhere pleasing."[10]

Amalendu Bose notes: "Years ago, while working in Bodley's library through several literary journals of the early Victorian period, I was agreeably surprised to come across repeated mention of the name of Kasiprasad Ghose, whose *The Shair and Other Poems* was the earliest work of Indian poetry in English to have been reviewed in England."[11]

The *Athenaeum* wrote a brief but commendatory notice in 1831. *New Monthly Magazine* wrote in June 1831: "Our new poet, Kasiprasad Ghose, describes himself as the 'first Hindoo who has ventured to publish a volume of English poems.' . . . The Shair (the Persian term for minstrel) is a poem of considerable length and of varied merit. . . . A great deal of poetic feeling may be discerned in parts of the poem."[12]

Another contemporary journal, *Fraser's Magazine*, wrote in its issue of November 1834, in the course of a brief notice of *Fisher's Drawing Room Scrap Book,* one of the Annuals of the age: "Of the engravings, we may particularly notice the picture of that amazingly clever lad, Khasiprasad (sic) Ghosh, the Hindoo poet,whose poem in honour of the

Gold River (Ganges) appears not only in Fisher's Scrap Book, but in Tom Roscos's Oriental Annual. Khasiprasad ought, therefore, to feel much honoured."[13]

Gooroo Churn Dutt (?-?) published *School Hours or Poems Composed At School* from Scott & Co., Calcutta in 1839. These poems were dedicated to D.L. Richardson in September 1838 and composed at Hindu College for "amusement and self-improvement." This collection is sometimes wrongly referred to as *Loyal Hours* by some bibliographers.[14]

D.L. Richardson's pupil, Rajnarain Dutt (1824-1839) published a book of poems titled *Osmyn: An Arabian Tale* in 1841, and dedicated the book to his teacher. In this book he attempted to tell an Arabian tale in English heroic couplets.

The early experiments in English poetry by H.L.V. Derozio, Kasiprasad Ghose and Rajnarain Dutt gradually built a tradition which was further consolidated by Michael Madhusudan Dutt (1824-1873). Highly westernized in his outlook, Madhusudan Dutt aspired in his early literary career to distinguish himself as a poet in English. He not only became a Christian and married two European ladies, but throughout his life, he zealously cultivated English ways and manners, and might justifiably claim to be "one of Macaulay's 'native Englishmen'."[15]

Being more gifted than Kasiprasad Ghose or Rajnarain Dutt, Madhusudan Dutt did not struggle through books of prosody but playfully wrote satires on his companions and epistles to his friends. Some of his poems he sent to the *Blackwood's Magazine,* dedicating them to William Wordsworth.

Madhusudan Dutt's English verses include two long poems, *The Captive Ladie* and *Visions of the Past,* some sonnets and a few lyrics, all of which he wrote before he left Madras for Calcutta in 1856.

A number of English verses written by Madhusudan Dutt during the Hindu College period were published in contemporary English periodicals like *The Bengal Spectator, Literary Gleaner, Calcutta Literary Gazette, Literary Blossom, Comet,* etc.[16] Dutt's poems of the Hindu College period were composed between 1841 and 1842 when the poet was just seventeen. It is interesting to know that the hymn sung by the congregation at the ceremony of conversion of Dutt at Old Mission Church of Mission Row, Calcutta on February 9, 1843, was composed by the poet himself.[17]

While in Madras since 1847, Dutt published his poems in *The Madras Circulator* under the pen-name of "Timothy Penpoem". He also chose a learned title for the series of his poems, DISJECTA MEMBRA POETAE, a phrase borrowed from one of the satires of Horace.

The Captive Ladie, Dutt's best known English poem, was written while he was working as a journalist, and was first published in the columns of the *Madras Circular* and *General Chronicle.* When it was later issued in a book form in 1849, it was accompanied by *Visions of the Past.* The *Athenaeum* declared about *The Captive Ladie* that the poem "contained poems which neither Scott nor Byron would have been ashamed to own."[18]

All the extant English poems of Madhusudan Dutt are now available in *Madhusudan Rachanavali* (The Works of Madhusudan), edited by Dr. Kshetra Gupta, published by Sahitya Samsad, Calcutta, in 1965.

In the annals of English poetry of Bengal the next poet is Soshee Chunder Dutt (1815-1885) who published several volumes of poetry from Calcutta, namely, *Miscellaneous Poems* (1848), *Stray Leaves* (1864) and *A Vision of Sumeru and Other Poems* (1878). The co-author of the last volume was Saurindra Mohun Tagore.[19] From a local English newspaper, we learn that "Soshee Chunder Dutt's 'Vision of Sumeru and Other Poems' was favourably received by the press of England and India."[20]

Together with his family, Govin Chunder Dutt (1828-1884) became a Christian, visited England, and published *The Dutt Family Album* in 1870 from Longmans, London. The book contains English verses by himself, his brothers and a cousin. The total number of poems in the book is 197: out of which 66 pieces are written by Govin Chunder Dutt, 73 by Omesh Chunder Dutt (1836-1912), 47 pieces by Greece Chunder Dutt (1833-1892), and rest 11 by Hur Chunder Dutt (1831-1901). M.K. Naik cites *The Dutt Family Album* as "the only instance of a family anthology in Indian English poetry." (36)

In the Preface to the *Album*, the joint authors (whose names do not appear anywhere in the book) state that "they venture on publication, not because they think their verse good, but in the hope that their book will be regarded, in some respects, as a curiosity. They are foreigners, natives of India of different ages, and in different walks of life, yet of one family."

Hur Chunder Dutt individually published a small volume of poems entitled *Fugitive Pieces* in 1851. Many of the poems from this book were later included in a larger volume called *Lotus Leaves* (1871).

Ishan Chunder Dutt (1818-1861) published *Essays and Poems* from Calcutta in 1872.

Greece Chunder Dutt went to England, and published his book of verse under the title *Cherry Blossom* in 1887. This book contains sonnets and lyrics on various subjects. The earlier Indian edition of this volume was called *Cherry Stones,* printed by P.S. D'Rozario & Co. in

1881. About this book, *The Statesman* commented: "*Cherry Stones* is a little book of smooth, flowing musical verse, consisting of sixty sonnets on many topics, ranging from the Burrabazar to the Revelation of St. John the Divine, and a series of miscellaneous pieces, forty-five in number, in many varieties of metre." (19 Nov. 1881)

Govin Chunder Dutt's eldest daughter Toru Dutt (1856-1877) along with her sister Aru Dutt (1854-1878) published a volume of English verse rendering of French poems under the title *A Sheaf Gleaned in French Fields* in 1876 from Saptahik Sambad Press, Bhowanipore, Calcutta. Encouraged by the warm critical appreciation accorded to this volume by English critics like Edmund Gosse, Toru Dutt composed original poems in English on Indian myths and legends. But since the poet breathed her last a year after, it was her father who collected and published the later poems in a volume entitled *Ancient Ballads and Legends of Hindustan* from Kegan Paul, London in 1882. The book carries an introductory memoir by Edmund Gosse.

Jotinder Mohan Tagore (1831-1908) brought out a book of poems under the title *Flights of Fancy* in 1881.

Nobo Kissan Ghose (1837-1918), under the pseudomym of Ram Sharma, published *Willow Drops* in 1873-74, *The Last Day: A Poem* in 1886, and *Shivaratri, Bhagaboti Gita and Miscellaneous Poems* in 1903. His *Poetical Works* was edited by D.C. Mallick, and published in 1919.

Dwijendralal Roy (1863-1913), the famous Bengali poet and patriot, published *The Lyrics of India* from Trubner & Co., London in 1886.

Manmohan Ghose (1869-1924), resident in England from 1878 to 1894, published five poems in an anthology called *Primavera* (1890) along with poems by Arthur Cripps, Laurence Binyon and Stephen Phillips. Oscar Wilde speaks of him as "the young Indian of brilliant scholarship and high literary attainment who gives some culture to Christ Church."[21]

In 1898 Manmohan Ghose published *Love Songs and Elegies* in Elkin Mathew's Shilling Garland series. In 1926, posthumously, a collection of his poems under the title *Songs of Love and Death,* edited by Laurence Binyon, was published by Basil Blackwell, Oxford.

In 1970 all the early poems of Ghose, that is, the poems written during the nineteenth century, were made available in *Collected Poems,* Vol. I, edited by his daughter Lotika Ghose, printed and published by Calcutta University. In 1974 Sahitya Akademi, New Delhi, brought out his *Selected Poems,* compiled by Lotika Ghose.

Manmohan Ghose's younger brother Aurobindo Ghose (1872-1950) is a prolific poet. But during the nineteenth century his output was meagre. During his stay in Baroda (1893-1906), he published *Songs of Myrtilla* from Lakshmi Vilas Printing Press, Baroda in 1895. Next year the same press printed his narrative poem, *Urvasie*. During this period, he completed *Love and Death*. His nineteenth-century lyrics, sonnets and long poems are now available in *Collected Poems*, published by Sri Aurobindo Ashram, Pondicherry in 1972.

During the glorious nineteenth century we come across another great personality, Swami Vivekananda (1863-1902), who composed highly moving poems in English which, however, saw the light of day as late as 1947.[22] His English poems are available in his *Complete Works*, Vol. IV, published by Advaita Ashram, Calcutta in 1955.

NOTES

1. Pallav Sengupta, *Kavi Derozio* (Bengali) (Calcutta, 1980), p. 23.
2. Susobhan Sarkar, Introduction, *Henry Derozio: Poems*, selected P. Lal (Calcutta, 1972), p. iii.
3. C. Paul Verghese, Preface, *Ibid.*, p. xix.
4. R.K. Dasgupta, Foreword, *Poems of Derozio*, ed. by F.B. Bradley-Birt (Calcutta, 1980), p. E.
5. Benoy Ghosh, *Bidrohi Derozio* (Bengali) (Calcutta, 1961).
6. Jogesh Chandra Bagol, *Derozio* (Bengali) (Calcutta, 1976).
7. R.C. Majumdar, *Renascent India, First Phase* (Calcutta, 1976).
8. Susobhan Sarkar, *On the Bengal Renaissance*, (Calcutta, 1979).
9. Debashish Bandopadhyaya, "Banedi Kolkatar Ghar-Bari" (Bengali) *Ananda Bazar Patrika*, Calcutta, 25 April 1982.
10. T.O.D. Dunn, *The Bengali Book of English Verse: A Record and An Appreciation* (Calutta, 1918), p. 5.
11. Amalendu Bose, "Some Poets of the Writers Workshop," *Critical Essays on Indian Writing in English*, ed. M.K. Naik, S.K. Desai and G.S. Amur (Dharwar, 1968), p. 31.
12. *Ibid.*
13. *Ibid.*, pp. 31-32.
14. V.K. Gokak ed., *The Golden Treasury of Indo-Anglian Poetry* (New Delhi, 1978), p. 272.
15. C. Paul Verghese, *Problems of the Indian Creative Writer in English* (Bombay, 1971), p. 18.
16. Amalendu Bose, *Michael Madhusudan Dutt* (New Delhi, 1961), p. 13.
17. *Ibid.*, p. 20.
18. Quoted by G. Parameswaran Pillai, *Representative Indians* (London, 1897), p. 70.
19. John B. Alphonso-Karkala, p. 110.

20. An Editorial note in *The Statesman*, November 19, 1881.
21. Oscar Wilde's review of *Primavera* in *Pall Mall Gazette*, qtd. Laurence Binyon, Introduction, *Songs of Love and Death* (London, 1926), p. 12.
22. M.K. Naik, p. 70.

The Bengal Renaissance

Let us now turn our attention to the major events of the Bengal Renaissance. By the end of the eighteenth century, Bengal witnessed in her social and cultural history a developing confrontation between the dark nadir of a progressive decline and a gradual blazing forth of a new light from the West. Eighteenth century may be named the Dark Age of Bengal before the nineteenth century burst forth upon her horizon. Soumyendra Nath Tagore graphically depicts this period of Bengal's history: "It was indeed the darkest period in modern Indian history. Old society and polity had crumbled and the ruins of an old social order lay scattered on all sides. As yet there was no force which could clear the debris and there was no attempt made to rebuild on the ancient foundations. Dead traditions, fossilised customs and irrational bigotry had choked the life-stream of the nation. Knowledge had been lost. It was a period of unrelenting darkness."[1]

In the words of H.M. Williams: "At the time of the East India Company's incursion, the Moghul Empire was in disarray and Hindu culture had sunk to a low level. There was not only a vacuum of power but a vacuum of culture."[2] K.R. Srinivasa Iyengar is of the same opinion: "India during the seventeenth and more especially the eighteenth century presented the spectacle of decay and misery unimaginable. . . . Vitality and the zest for life were at a vanishing point, spirituality glowed but in fitful embers, and all intellectual activity was nearly at a standstill. By the end of the eighteenth century, India was to all appearance a Waste Land."[3]

Nemai Sadhan Bose remarks: "Actually the eighteenth century, particularly the later half of it, was one of the darkest ages in the long and eventful history of India."[4] With the decline of the Mughal empire India lost her political unity. The later Mughals were weak and unworthy rulers. They were exploited by the nobles who constantly engaged themselves in intrigues and conspiracies and other corrupt activities. The French traveller Jean Law stated in 1759: "I have travelled everywhere from Bengal to Delhi, but nowhere have I found anything from anyone except oppression of the poor and plundering of wayfarers. . . . The Indian nobles are a set of disorderly, inconsistent blockheads, who exist solely for ruining a world of people."[5]

As a result, in every sphere of life in Bengal, there was either stagnation or decay. R.C. Majumder remarks: "It would be hardly any exaggeration to say that higher education in Bengal, both among the Hindus and the Muslims, followed a stereo-typed course during the half millennium ending in 1800 A.D."[6] He further states: "Higher education consisted in transmitting knowledge of religion or orthodox principles as was the practice hundreds of years ago. India practically stood still where it was six hundred years ago." (32)

For female education there was no public institution as there prevailed a superstitious idea that if a girl was taught how to read and write, she would become a widow soon after marriage.

The practice of *sati* or burning of a widow along with the dead body of her husband is a flagrant example of how callous the Hindu society was towards women. In Calcutta and its neighbourhood alone there were 153, 289 and 441 cases of *Sati*, respectively, in 1815, 1816 and 1817.[7]

Another glaring example of the Hindu society's inhuman and superstitious customs was witnessed during the annual *Charak Puja*, when men, sometimes with iron pikes or arrows inserted in various parts of their bodies, were tied to a rope which was attached to a wheel, high up in the air, supported by a bamboo, and as the wheel was whirled around, the rope snapped, and the bodies were thrown to a distance, reduced to a shapeless mass. This horrible game reminds us of the cruelties inflicted upon the prisoners of war in Roman Empire.

Another typical social evil was the marriage of bridegrooms of *Kulin Brahmins* (the class of priests of higher social prestige) to a large number of brides, "not unoften as many as fifty or sixty and sometimes even hundred or more."[8] This led to several corrupt practices: one of them being the incident of marriage of several girls simultaneously to an old *Kulin Brahmin,* just to remove their spinsterhood which was considered a social ignominy.

From a study of the superstitious customs prevalent in Bengal during the eighteenth century, it appears that the Hindu society reached a complete paralysis of moral sensibilities and lack of human feelings and compassion. The Hindus blindly followed the injunctions imposed by the age-old *Shastras* as interpreted by the corrupt motivated Brahmins. Hence reason and free judgement were nowhere to be found in the activities of the Bengalis during this Dark Age. R.C. Majumdar has rightly remarked: "The Hindu society had not materially changed from what it was in the thirteenth century A.D." (33)

Dwarkanath Tagore ascribed the reasons for Hindu decadence to Mohammedan conquest in a letter dated December 6, 1838 to the Englishman: "The present characteristic failings of natives are want of truth, a want of integrity, a want of independence. These were not the characteristics of former days, before the religion was corrupted and education had disappeared. It is to the Mohammedan conquest that these evils are owing and they are the invariable results of the loss of liberty and national degradation. The Mohammedans introduced in this country all the vices of an ignorant, intolerant and licentious soldiery. The utter destruction of learning and science was an invariable part of their system, and the conquered, no longer able to protect their lives by arms and independence, fell into opposite extremes of abject submission, deceit and fraud. Such has been the condition of the Natives of Hindustan for centuries."[9]

As the Muslim was disintegrating, the British, who had come to India as merchants, took the opportunity to turn into rulers. In the Battle of Plassey in 1757, Clive routed Siraj-ud-daulah, and paved the way for the British conquest and administration of Bengal. Though on the one hand, the scene was chaotic and disorderly; on the other, with the advent of the British, a new order of things was slowly emerging. To quote Saumyendranath Tagore: "The West, heralded by Britain, had come to India not merely as an agent of commerce, but as an instrument of history, destined to shake India out of her stupor and to release a new tide of thought and activity in the old river-bed of her history." (8) According to M.K. Naik, the new rulers were "instrumental in planting the seeds of a modernization process in the eighteenth century Indian Waste Land—seeds which started burgeoning in the nineteenth century."[10]

The establishment of the new Council and Supreme Court in Calcutta and the appointment of Warren Hastings as the Governor-General in 1774 made the Bengalis aware of the change in political authority. During the next twenty-five years the British supremacy in Bengal became an established fact, and this was recognised to be so by the people of Bengal.

The Bengalis welcomed the British rule for they believed that the British would bring them peace, prosperity and security. After 600 years or more of Mohammedan rule, the Bengalis got the opportunity to worship their gods in their temples free from sacrilege and destruction.

The attitude of the Bengalis towards the British during the early part of the nineteenth century may be evident from the petition that Raja Rammohan Roy wrote to the King in Council in 1823: "the Natives of Bengal wanting vigour of body, and adverse to active exertion, remained during the whole period of the Muhammedan conquest, faithful to the existing Government, although their property was often plundered, their religion insulted and their blood wantonly shed. Divine Providence, at last, in its abundant mercy, stirred up the English nation to break the yoke of those tyrants, and to receive the oppressed Natives of Bengal under its protection."[11] Rammohan Roy's final Appeal to the Christian Public is also relevant in this context: "I now conclude my Essay by offering up thanks to the Supreme Disposer of events of this universe, for having unexpectedly delivered this country from the long-continued tyranny of its former Rulers, and placed it under the Government of the English: a nation who not only were blessed with the enjoyment of civil and political liberty, but also interested themselves in promoting liberty and social happiness, as well as free enquiry into literary and religious subjects, among those nations to which their influence extends."[12]

The change that was ushered in was phenomenal. In course of the nineteenth century a total transformation of Bengali psyche took place. Here is a sketch of the main events that brought about this change. First there grew a high standard of rational thinking that motivated several religious and social reforms. The Bengal Renaissance brought about a revolution in the growth of Bengali literature, too. People became proud of their nationality, and a wave of patriotic feelings swept over the whole country resulting in the formation of political organizations and movements that stressed intense nationalism and deep patriotism. R.C. Majumdar rightly concludes: "there were such remarkable developments in religious, social and political ideas, and wonderful growth in literature with a liberal outlook on men and things, broadened by a knowledge of the outside world, that it may be said without exaggeration that Bengal had passed from the Medieval to the Modern Age." (259)

The first cause of this transformation is the impact of English education which broke the barriers of the parochial studies and opened the floodgates of Western ideas. C. Paul Verghese goes so far as to say: "English education was not merely a catalyst but was mainly instrumental in bringing about this renaissance."[13] That is why Sir Jadunath Sarkar describes the Indian Renaissance as "the greatest gift of the English."[14] Percival Spear comments: "The British were the harbingers of the West. At times unconsciously, at times with optimistic zeal, and at times with reluctance or dislike, they were the vehicles of Western influence . . . the British provided the bridge for India to pass from the medieval world of the Mughuls to the new age of science and humanism."[15]

The East India Company initially did not want to interfere in the educational systems of their newly won country. It is the Christian Missionaries who first undertook to spread English education far and wide in Bengal. As far back as in 1731, a free school was started by St. Andrew's Presbyterian Church, and a small number of pupils were taught English and modern subjects by a few other missionary organizations.

In 1814, Rev. Robart May founded a free school in his own house; in course of time he established altogether sixteen schools, some of which were in villages, with a total enrolment of 951 pupils.

The Christian Missionaries, Carey, Marshman and Ward founded the Baptist Mission College at Serampore in 1818. They also founded several schools. The Lord Bishop of Calcutta established a college in 1820. Rev. Alexander Duff founded the General Assembly's Institution in Calcutta in 1830. Later, when Duff and his colleagues left the General Assembly of the Church of Scotland and joined the Free Church of Scotland, they founded another college named after it. In June 1906 the two institutions were united under the name of Scottish Church College. St. Xavier's College was founded in 1860. St. Paul's Cathedral Mission College was founded in 1865. Loreto sisters established Loreto House in Calcutta in 1842. Rev. William Macfarlane founded Scottish Universities Mission College at Kalimpong in 1886. St. Joseph's College grew out of St. Xavier's Day School, Calcutta, founded more than a century ago. All these missionary English education and Western culture among the Bengalis during the nineteenth century.

The Christian missionaries' activities were, however, not restricted to the diffusion of English education alone. They found the liberal education imparted through these English schools and colleges a fruitful means of converting Hindus to Christianity as this education made the Hindus aware of the superstitious accretions in their idolatrous religion. A Christian missionary remarked that Indians "now engaged in the degrading and polluting worship of idols, shall be brought to the knowledge of the true God, and Jesus Christ whom He has sent."[16] Thus we find that with the spread of English education, Christianity percolated into the life of Bengali Hindus, as several members of well-known Bengali families embraced Christianity. The most notable cases of conversion were those of Michael Madhusudan Dutt and several members of the Dutt family of Rambagan.

The year 1817 is a landmark in the history of English education in Bengal. In this year Calcutta School Book Society was established, and managed by such eminent persons as Sir Edward Hyde East, J.H. Harrington, W.B. Bailey, William Carey, Tarinicharan Mitra, Radhakanta Dev and Ramkamal Sen. The Society was maintained by the donations of both Englishmen and Indians. The Society undertook to prepare, print, publish and distribute either free or at a cheap price suitable text-books in English and vernaculars for schools. This Society established Calcutta School Society in 1818 with David Hare as its European secretary and Radhakanta Dev as its Indian secretary. The Society's objective and function was to help and improve the existing schools in Calcutta and establish more schools according to need, and also establish institutions for higher education so that students passing from schools might pursue their education further and make themselves suitable as teachers for the schools under its administration.

The more important event of 1817 was the establishment of Hindu College in Calcutta. Under the patronage of Sir Hyde East, the then Chief Justice of Supreme Court, and the active inspiration and co-operation of David Hare, Rammohan Roy, and several respectable Hindus of rank and wealth, the college was founded. Sir Hyde East, who held a meeting in his house in connection with the proposal for the establishment of such a college, wrote to the Earl of Buckinghamshire in a letter dated 17 May 1816: "The principal objects proposed for the adoption of the meeting were the cultivation of the Bengali and English languages in particular . . . the English system of morals. . . , and in time, as the fund increases, English belles lettres, poetry etc."[17] The Hindu College became a distinguished seat of learning with several outstanding European teachers in its faculties and produced, in several numbers, the geniuses that made the Bengal Renaissance possible.

The establishment of the Hindu College was followed by that of a large number of institutions, both in and outside Calcutta, for teaching English and imparting a system of liberal education.

In 1836, Mr. H.H. Wilson, one of the members of the Hindu College Governing Body, stated that when he left Calcutta "there were about 6000 youths studying English."[18]

In 1835 the British Government ultimately announced its educational policy which would further the cause of English education in Bengal. The pressure of the "Anglicists," already referred to in the first chapter, was instrumental in disposing the Government's policy in favour of English education. Raja Rammohan Roy's spirited appeal to Lord Amherst in favour of English education is already quoted. The cause of the "Anglicists" was further strengthened by the timely arrival of Thomas Babington Macaulay, the Law Member (1834-1838) in the Governor-General's Supreme Council in India, and his appointment as the Chairman of the Committee of Public Instruction. Macaulay wrote a long Minute on Indian Education which persuaded Lord Bentinck to pass the resolution of the British Government on March 7, 1835 to spend Government's educational funds on English education alone.

John B. Alphonso-Karkala rightly points out: "Although the introduction of English education in India in the beginning of the nineteenth century can be attributed to the early Christian missionary enterprise, its extension was largely due to the historic decision of 1835."[19]

Another historic event took place in 1857. In this year the University of Calcutta was established with Lord Canning as its first Chancellor; and the first fellows of the Calcutta University were Prasanna Kumar Tagore, Ramprosad Roy, Moulavi Mohammad Wajeeh, Iswarchandra Vidyasagar and Ramgopal Ghose. The foundation of the University marked the culmination of Western education in Bengal; and Western education caused a rapid growth in the number of English-educated Bengalis.

The English education and Western culture made Bengalis keenly conscious of the retrogressive effects of the superstitious customs that were so far prevalent in the society under the various injunctions and dogmas issued by the Hindu Shastras. This consciousness gave birth to several religions and social reforms. The mighty reformers like Rammohan Roy, Derozio and Vidyasagar brought about drastic changes in social customs. The leading reform was the abolition of the *Sati* or the burning of the living widow on the funeral pyre of her dead husband. A total of about 8000 burnings were officially recorded between 1815 and 1828.[20] Between 1818 and 1829 Rammohan Roy wrote three tracts in fiery condemnation of this murderous practice. When Lord Bentinck finally abolished the *Sati* by a legislation on December 4, 1829, a public petition signed by 300 Hindus, under the leadership of Rammohan Roy, was sent to the Governor-General, thanking him for this kind measure. Rammohan Roy also arranged a petition to the Parliament to prevent any repeal of Lord Bentinck's order.

Another social custom of throwing the first baby born to a woman who had remained barren for a considerable period of time after her marriage into the Ganges was prohibited by the Regulation VI of 1802.

Vidyasagar raised his voice against child-marriage and strongly campaigned against polygamy. In 1855 he caused a sensation by advocating widow-marriage in the teeth of strong orthodox hostility. His lifelong untiring efforts resulted in the legislation of widow-marriage by Hindu Widow's Remarriage Act (Act XV of 1856).

The other social reform, in which Vidyasagar along with Drinkwater Bethune took a leading part, was the promotion of female education which was so far a social taboo.

The advent of the British and the introduction of English education was responsible not only for the rationalisation of thinking and behaviour leading to various religious and social reforms among the Bengalis but also for the re-discovery of the glory that was India. It is the great British Orientalists who drew the attention of the Indians to the rich cultural heritage of India. This new awareness of India's glorious past played a significant role in bringing about the Bengal Renaissance. Jawaharlal Nehru has rightly observed that the awakening of India "was two-fold: she looked to the West and, at the same time, she looked at herself and her own past."[21] Dilip Kumar Biswas has commented: "The classical past of India was a source of inspiration to the Indian Renaissance."[22]

In the re-discovery of India's past, some of the early officials of the East India Company played a significant role. Sir William Jones, H.T. Coleridge, James Prinsep, and Bothlingk were some such Orientalists who contributed a great deal to the revival of ancient Indian culture.

Sir William Jones (1746-1794) founded the Royal Asiatic Society of Bengal in Calcutta in 1784 to promote Asiatic studies. He studied Sanskrit and translated into English Sanskrit classics like *Sakuntala, Hitopadesa,* the *Enchanted Fruit,* and parts of the *Vedas* and *Manu.* K.R. Srinivasa Iyengar remarks that Sir William Jones set in motion currents of thought that helped "the Indian renaissance to its fruitful blossoming in the fullness of time."[23]

The archaelogical explorations and excavations in several parts of India under the supervision of Alexander Cunningham, and the writings of Max Muller, Wilson, Fergusson and Rajendralal Mitra in a popular form brought home to the people of India that their motherland in ancient times was no less civilised than Greece or Rome. The European scholars discovered and wrote in their books about the fact that the Hindus belong to the same group of forefathers from which originated the famous Europeans. They further averred that the ancient Hindu scriptures, the *Vedas,* were the oldest literary works of the world, and the *Upanishads* contained the most profound speculations of the human mind. The great administrative capacity and humanitarian benevolence of Emperor Asoka who ruled the whole of India and Afghanistan together, and the sway of Buddhism over a large portion of the population of the world were new facts revealed to inspire the mind of the Bengalis with a renewed spirit of self-confidence. This led to a spirit of nationalism and ardent patriotism. R.C. Majumdar aptly notes: "The revelation of India's past was one of the strongest foundations in which Indian nationalism was built."[24]

The role of the great Bengalis like Raja Rammohan Roy, and the other later members of the *Brahmo Samaj* like Keshub Chandra Sen and Debendranath Tagore, and the savants like Ramakrishna Paramhamsa and his dynamic disciple Vivekananda in re-discovering the rich heritage of India, and in imbuing and urging the people of Bengal with self-confidence, self-respect, nationalism and patriotism cannot be underestimated.

Bipin Chandra Pal records that Bankim Chandra Chatterjee "openly attempted a re-examination, a re-interpretation and re-adjustment of our old theology and ethics in the light of the most advanced modern thought and in accordance with the new rules of literary criticism and scriptural interpretation that had been so powerfully influencing current religious life and thought in Christendom itself."[25]

While Bankim Chandra Chatterjee defended Hinduism theoretically, Ramakrishna Paramhamsa demonstrated through his *sadhana* that the enlightenment as laid down in the ancient Hindu scriptures, both Vedic and post-vedic, were valid even in modern times. He, however, stressed that all religions were true and pure in essence, and would lead to salvation, if properly pursued.

It was, however, left to great Swami Vivekananda to preach the pristine precepts of the Hindu scriptures to the world. His address at the Chicago Parliament of Religions in 1893 in the presence of representatives of almost all the religions of the world is monumental. It brought about a change in the attitude of the Western people towards the Hindu religion. The Western people so far regarded Hinduism as a bundle of superstitions, immoralities and untenable dogmas, not suitable for the progressive world of today. After listening to Vivekananda's most cogent and illuminating exposition of the lofty principles of Hinduism, they approved of Hinduism with open-hearted enthusiasm.

After his return to India, Vivekananda travelled throughout India, literally from Kanyakumari to Kashmir, addressing innumerable public meetings, at which he stressed the spiritual basis of the Hindu civilization and asked the youths to sacrifice their lives for the common good of all. His teachings parmeated the life and activities of all the great nationalists and martyrs who sacrificed their all and even embraced death for the liberation of India.

Though the Indian National Congress was formed in 1885, and continuous uprisings against the British government took place towards the end of the nineteenth century, the seeds of freedom movements were laid in the minds of the Bengalis as far back as the days of Raja Rammohan Roy and Derozio. Passionate love of liberty made Raja Rammohan Roy "take interest in, and deeply sympathise with, all political movements all over the world that had for their object the advancement of popular freedom."[26]

But more manifest expression of love of India with intense patriotic zeal was to be found in Derozio's poetry:

To India—My Native Land

My country, in thy day of glory past
A beauteous halo circled round thy brow,
And worshipped as a deity thou wast.
Where is that glory, where that reverence now?
Thy eagle pinion is chained down at last,
And grovelling in the lowly dust art thou:
Thy minstrel hath no wreath to weave for thee
Save the sad story of thy misery,
Well—let me dive into the depths of time,
And bring from out the ages that have rolled
A few small fragments of those wrecks sublime,
Which human eye may never more behold;
And let the guerdon of my labour be
My fallen country, one kind wish from thee.[27]

R.C. Majumdar regards this poem of Derozio, published in 1927, as "the first patriotic poem written in India."(289) Derozio instilled in the minds of his students the love of freedom, faith in the history and revolutionary philosophy of France, and a deep interest in the wave of revolutions in Europe in 1830. That his students looked forward to the outbreak of similar revolutions in India may be gathered from the series of essays that they published on the grievances of India in the *Bengal Harukaru* of 1843.

B.B. Majumdar cites the poetry of Kasiprasad Ghose as "the first cry of patriotic fervour which was roused in Bengal by the introduction of western culture":

But woe me, I never shall live to behold
That day of thy triumph, when firmly and bold,
Thou shalt mount on the wings of an eagle on high
To the region of knowledge and blest liberty.[28]

The makers of the Bengal Renaissance inculcated and fostered a profound spirit of intense nationalism and patriotism throughout the nineteenth century through their writings, speeches and activities that inspired and moulded the minds of Chittaranjan Das, Subhas Chandra Bose, Bipin Chandra Pal, Surendranath Bannerjee and Sri Aurobindo, to name a few among the great revolutionaries of Bengal, who, along with the patriots and revolutionaries in the rest of the country, shook and threw the British imperialists from their seats of power in India finally in 1947.

An analysis of the major trends of events that took place in the nineteenth-century Bengal reveals four chief characteristics of the Bengal Renaissance: (a) an over-all love of English education and Western culture with a partial acceptance of Christianity as a form of worship; (b) an intense zeal and determined efforts for the abolition of superstitious customs and introduction of several social reforms; (c) an all-out effort to re-discover the rich cultural heritage and the glorious chapters of India's past history; (d) a spirit of intense nationalism and patriotism inspiring every thought and action of the leaders of the Bengal Renaissance.

In the following chapters I intend to analyse the nineteenth-century English poetry of Bengal with a view to tracing in it the reflection of the above-mentioned characteristics of the Bengal Renaissance. Let me conclude this chapter by quoting from Rabindranath Tagore:

> The following anthology (*A Bengali Book of English Verse*) has its greatest interest in being the self-recording evidence of the earliest response that Bengal gave to the touch of the West. I can safely assert that she is the only country in the Orient which has shown any distinct indication of being thrilled by the voice of Europe as it came through her literature. . . . Bengal was stirred by the force of new ideas breaking in upon her from the Western horizon. . . . The shock which roused Bengal mainly came through literature and a great part of its energy followed the same channel of literature for its expression.[29]

NOTES

1. Saumyendranath Tagore, *Raja Rammohan Roy* (New Delhi, 1977), p. 7.
2. H.M. Williams, *Indo-Anglian Literature* (Madras, 1976), p. 13.
3. K.R. Srinivasa Iyengar, *Indian Writing in English* (New Delhi, 1983), p. 23.
4. Nemai Sadhan Bose, *Indian Awakening and Bengal* (Calcutta, 1976), p. 1.
5. *Ibid.*
6. R.C. Majumdar, *History of the Freedom Movement of India* (Calcutta, 1971),Vol. I, p. 32
7. *Ibid.*, p. 34.

8. *Ibid.*, p. 35.
9. Qtd. Kishorichand Mitra, *Memoirs of Dwarkanath Tagore* (Calcutta), p. 60.
10. M.K. Naik, *A History of Indian English Literature* (New Delhi, 1982), p. 8.
11. *The English Works of Raja Rammohan Roy*, ed. Nag and Burman (Calcutta, 1958), pp. 445-46.
12. *Ibid.*, p. 874.
13. C. Paul Verghese, *Problems of the Indian Creative Writer in English* (Bombay, 1971), p. 14.
14. Jadunath Sarkar, *India through the Ages* (Calcutta, 1962), p. 57.
15. Percival Spear, *The Oxford History of Modern India* (New Delhi, 1978), pp. 6-7.
16. *Calcutta Journal*, March 11, 1822.
17. Qtd. R.C. Majumdar, *Renascent India* (Calcutta, 1976), p. 34.
18. *Ibid.*, p. 40.
19. John B. Alphonso-Karkala, *Indo-English Literature in the Nineteenth Century* (Mysore, 1970), p. 11.
20. Susobhan Sarkar, *On the Bengal Renaissance* (Calcutta, 1979), p. 17.
21. Jawaharlal Nehru, *The Discovery of India* (Bombay, 1961), pp. 330-31.
22. Dilip Kumar Biswas, "Maharshi Debendranath Tagore and the Tattvabodhini Sabha," *Studies in the Bengal Renaissances,* ed. Atul Chandra Gupta (Calcutta, 1958), p. 38.
23. K.R. Srinivasa Iyengar, *The Indian Contribution to Engish Literature* (Bombay, 1945), pp. 2-3.
24. R.C. Majumdar, *History of the Freedom Movement of India,* Vol. I, p. 291.
25. B.C. Pal, *Memoirs of My Life and Times* (Calcutta, 1973), Vol. II, p. 426.
26. *The English Works of Raja Rammohan Roy*, (Allahabad, 1906), pp. 287-88.
27. H.L.V. Derozio, *Poems*, ed. Bradley-Birt, p. 2.
28. B.B. Majumdar, *History of Political Thought from Rammohan to Dayananda* (Calcutta, 1934), pp. 85-86.
29. Rabindranath Tagore, Foreword, *A Bengali Book of English Verse*, ed. T.O.D. Dunn (London, 1918), p. 1.

The Impact of English Education

The impact of English education on the nineteenth-century English poetry of Bengal is detectable in its twin aspects: namely, first, the influence of British poetry, and second, the influence of the religious ideas of Christianity.

English education brought the Bengali poets into contact with the poets of England whose poetry books used to be imported into the city of Calcutta regularly both for the college libraries and the personal libraries of the Europeans and the Bengali aristocrats.

With the propagation of English education, the infiltration of Christianity as a religion among the Bengalis also took place. Under the influence of English education and Western culture, a sizable number of enlightened Bengalis, particularly from the upper middle class families, took a fancy to Christianity as a liberating agent which provided them with a route of escape from the Hindu superstitions and dogmas. Thus both the literature and religion of England fascinated the Bengali poets writing in English, and exercised a considerable influence on their creative output.

In this chapter I will trace both the influences in the poetry of successive Bengali poets writing in English during the nineteenth century.

First, I will consider the influence of the poetry of England. To start with, let me quote R.C. Majumdar: "The contact with English literature and, through it, with that of other Western countries, may be regarded as one of the greatest contributing factors to the Renaissance in India in the nineteenth century. For it revolutionized the attitude of English-knowing Indians to life and literature and inaugurated an altogether new phase in Indian literature."[1] Majumdar particularly points to Romantic literature that caused a "sea-change" in Bengali poetry. The comment is no less relevant to the nineteenth-century English poetry of Bengal: "The influence of Romantic literature in Europe changed its [Bengali poetry's] whole character, and individual emotions as well as social and political topics formed its main theme."[2]

Reviewing the impact of English literature on Indians of the Renaissance period, K.M. Munshi has remarked: "English literature of the nineteenth century provided new inspiration to the university men in India who took to Shakespeare and Scott, Byron, Shelley and Keats . . . with avid enthusiasm."[3] We also find the trace of the influence of Milton, Moore and Campbell in the nineteenth century English poetry of Bengal.

H.M. Williams has rightly pointed out: "contact with British life and literature inevitably brought poetry to India, the poetry of Wordsworth, Scott, Shelley, Keats, Byron. In the explosive influence of English culture, romanticism played an important part."[4]

V.K. Gokak puts the same idea metaphorically: "Indo-Anglian poetry was born under a Romantic star. It learned to lisp in the manner of Byron and Scott in the verse of Derozio, M.M. Dutt and others. It began with verse-romances and lyrics written in the Romantic vein."[5]

M.K. Naik makes an assessment of the Indians' taste in poetry during the nineteenth century: "Both the 'Romantic gold-standard' in Stephen Spender's phrase and its diluted Victorian version continued to dominate Indian verse in English for a very long time. That this was so because Indo-Anglian poetry arose during the heyday of Romanticism is obvious enough. The part played by the popularity of F.T. Palgrave's *The Golden Treasury* in this process needs to be emphasized. The selection influenced not only early Indo-Anglian poets but also the new poets in Indian languages."[6]

Writing specifically about Derozio, K.R. Srinivasa Iyengar observes: "As a poet, Derozio was obviously influenced by the Romantics—notably Byron, Scott, Moore; but he knew his Shelley and Keats also very well."[7] The influence of the Romantic poets is manifest in Derozio's love of Nature.

H.M. Williams estimates the extent of the Romantic influence on Derozio: "Derozio submitted himself completely to English romantic influences." (15) According to him: "The essence of his poetic sensibility is a melancholy and reflective, occasionally passionate, romanticism of Man and nature, derived principally from Byron and Wordsworth." (16) Williams gives Derozio the position of a pioneer "in expressing a romantic reaction to tropical nature, on the model of Byron and the English lake-poets."

A.N. Dwivedi is of the same opinion: Derozio "wrote mostly under the spell of Lord Byron and Thomas Moore. His published work, *The Fakir of Jungheera and Other Poems* . . . is full of Byronic echoes."[8]

M.K. Naik specifies the poems of Derozio which obviously echo some British poets: "The shorter poems [of Derozio] show a strong influence of British romantic poems in theme (e.g. 'Sonnet: To the Moon'; 'The Golden Vase'; 'Sonnet: Death, my Best Friend'), sentiment, imagery and diction, with some traces of neo-classicism (e.g. 'The heart . . . where hope eternal springs,' with its obvious echo of Pope). His satirical verse (e.g. 'Don Juanics') and the long narrative poems (*The Fakeer of Jungheera*) clearly indicate his special affinity with Byron."[9]

John B. Alphonso-Karkala points out Derozio's affinity with the eighteenth-century British poets: "In his 'prologue' to the play which his school was producing, he imitated the rhymed couplet of the late eighteenth-century English poets. Presenting the members of the dramatic company, he compares the inexperienced actors to 'new fledged birds . . . unus'd to soar.'"[10]

Though C.Paul Verghese criticises Derozio for the derivative quality of his poetry, he does not fail to assess his true position: "However, it should be said to his credit that he was the first Indian to attempt to write romantic poetry in English."[11]

From Susobhan Sarkar we come to know of the influence of another British poet on Derozio: "It may safely be conjectured that Derozio derived from Drummond his taste in literature and philosophy, his love of Burns."[12]

C. Paul Verghese considers most of the themes of Derozio's poetry to be an echo of English romantic poets' favourite topics: "Even in the expression of high ideals of liberty, freedom and patriotism, let alone his wistfulness, obsession with death and mood of escapism, he [Derozio] echoed his Romantic masters." (xxiii)

E.W. Madge, an early biographer of Derozio, remarks on the influence of the poets who were popular in the days of Derozio: "The brilliant hues of the Byronic sunset flung their glow over Derozio's sky. His style has been termed the echo of Byron, Moore and L.E. Landon. But these were the literary idols of the day, and it may well be understood that to break away from fashionable models would for a youthful and inexperienced writer only spell disaster."[13]

Derozio's poetry presents a very fine illustration of the influence of English education. Taking Bradley-Birt's edition of his poems as our text, we can start with the first poem, "The Harp of India." The first line of the poem, "Why hang'st thou lonely on yon withered bough?"[14] echoes both the sentiment and rhythm of Keats' poem "La Belle Dame Sans Merci":

> O, what can ail thee, knight-at-arms,
> Alone and palely loitering?
> The sedge has withered from the lake,
> And no birds sing.[15]

The words "alone" and "withered" are clearly assimilated by Derozio in his poem verbatim, and the concept of "no birds sing" is reflected in the image of the "unstrung" harp.

The poem titled "My Dream" is a repository of romantic images. The following lines by Derozio

> Was it thy spirit came to me
> To visit me in sleep? . . .
> Not half so sweet the nightingale
> Unto the rosebud sings,
> As came thy voice of other days,
> With which my ear still rings. (3)

remind us of Shelley's poem "The Indian Serenade":

> I arise from dreams of thee,
> And a spirit in my feet
> Hath led me—who knows how?
> To thy chamber window, Sweet: . . .
> The nightingale's complaint,
> It dies upon her heart;
> As I must on thine,
> Oh, beloved as thou art.[16]

The poem "The Maniac Widow" is romantic in vision and description. The following lines by Derozio

> That wreath I'll weave of flowrets rare,
> And bind it around his forehead fair,
> Anemones, roses, and lilies white,
> With cypress twigs, and the flower of night. (5)

are reminiscent of the flower-stanza of Keats' poem "Ode to a Nightingale":

> White hawthorn, and the pastoral eglantine;
> Fast fading violets covered up in leaves;
> And mid-May's eldest child,
> The coming musk-rose. (208)

Derozio's glorification of love, as illustrated in the following excerpt from the poem "Song," recalls Shelley's idealization of love:

Oh! there's the hallowed charm that brings
    Such solace to the dove,
And that alone's the spell that makes
    Her life a life of love. (15)

The poem entitled "The Tomb" embodies Derozio's obsession with death. The following lines

'Tis where woe is all forgotten
    And the riven heart is blest;
Where the wicked cease from troubling
    And the weary are at rest. (27)

recall Keats' lines about death in his poem "Ode to a Nightingale":

for many a time
I have been half in love with easeful Death,
Called him soft names in many a mused rhyme,
    To take into the air my quiet breath. (208)

Derozio's poem "The Bridal" is a romantic ballad, written in imitation of Keats' narrative poems like "The Eve of St. Agnes" and "Isabella."

The first few lines of "Evening in August" recalls several features of the Nature poems of Wordsworth:

Roll on, fair Ganges:—what a noble stream!
And on its bosom the last, lingering beam
Of the red, setting sun serenely lies,
Smiling, like Hope's last ray—and then it dies!
And O! the clouds—what colours they display,
Sport for a while, then melt in air away! (34)

The graphic description of the various details of Nature along with the poet's tendency to humanize the objects of nature, as illustrated in phrases like "noble stream," and "like Hope's last ray," indicate the influence of Wordsworth's poem "Tintern Abbey."

"Song of the Indian Girl" presents the theme of transitoriness of dream and hope:

My dream was bright, but it past away,
    The thought so sweet is gone

And hope hath fled, like a rainbow's ray,
Or a beam of the setting sun! (40)

The influence of Shelley's and Keats' poems is detectable in Derozio's choice of such a theme.

Derozio might have derived his inspiration for dealing with Greek characters and incidents in his poems from the Hellenic interests of Shelley and Keats. Derozio's poems like "Thermopylae," "Greece," "The Greeks at Marathon," "Address to the Creeks," "Phyle," "Sonnet—Where Are Thy Waters, Lethe?" bear witness to the poet's preoccupation with Greek themes.

Derozio's frequent references to, and elaborate treatment of, images from nature may be traced to the influence of the Romantic poets. Most of his poems use images, similes and metaphors from the world of nature. Some of them are even no more than plain descriptions of nature in its varied forms which have inspired certain perceptions and feelings in the heart of the poet. Wordsworth, Coleridge, Byron, Shelley and Keats have all cast influence upon the poetry of Derozio, but through the analysis of his poetry, it may be found out to which poets he is particularly indebted.

"To the Dog Star" has the following lines:

How the Chaldeen watched thee, brightest star!
Brightest, and loveliest in the vault of heaven! (48)

whose ideas and style echo the ideal and image in Keats' sonnet,

Bright star! would I were steadfast as thou art
Not in lone splendour hung aloft the night. (372)

"Yorick's Skull," by its very title, reminds us of the grave-digging scene in Shakespeare's *Hamlet.* The octave of the sonnet underlines the fragility of human life:

It is a most humiliating thought,
That man, who deems himself the lord of all,
(Alas! why doth he thus himself miscall?)
Must one day turn to nought, or worse than nought;
Despite of all his glory, he must fall
Like a frail leaf in autumn. (55)

Derozio further writes:

> This is a lesson for thee, Pride! (55)

which is reminiscent of the conclusion of Shelley's sonnet "Ozymandias."

"Morning after a Storm" recalls both Shelley and Wordsworth. The following lines echo Shelley's poem "Ode to the West Wind":

> The hamlet was in desolation laid
> By the strong spirits of the storm; there lay
> Around me many a branch of giant trees,
> Scattered as leaves are by the southern breeze
> Upon a brook, on an autumnal day. (56)

The general ambience of the description of nature along with the sentiment expressed in the next few lines of the above poem is not only Wordsworthian but carries an expression "How leapt my young heart" which reminds us of Wordsworth's poem "My heart leaps up."

The long narrative poem "Ada" abounds in romantic images. Further, the name of the poem is the name of Byron's daughter whom Byron mentions in *Childe Harold*, Canto III. The following lines chosen at random from the poem indicate the influence of the Romantic poets:

> Lady my bark is floating by,
> And the moonbeam is soft as thine own blue eye;
> And the breeze that breathes is fresh and light
> O'er the waves that dance in the moonbeam bright! (62)
>
> 'Twas beautiful!—The lake's blue wave
> That girt the island, and did lave
> It's banks, flowed making music o'er
> The pebbles that lay on the shore. (64)
>
> And, in her eye the tear is bright,
> Like dew on violets by night. (67)

Derozio's images are a mixture of images used by the Romantic poets like Wordsworth, Byron, Shelley and Keats.

In this connection, it may be mentioned that Derozio was very fond of Byron's poetry which accounts for Derozio's choice of Byronic lines as epigraphs for several of his poems. For example, poems like "Phyle" and "Sappho" have epigraphs from Byron. The poem "Leaves" has an epigraph from Shelley.

However, a comparison between a poem by a British Romantic poet and a poem by Derozio will reveal that though Derozio has been influenced by the romantic love of nature, he has not been able to assimilate the British Romantic poet's capacity to crystallize a romantic feeling in an evocative image. A comparison between a few lines from Derozio's poem "Night" and Shelley's poem "To Night" will throw light on this. Derozio's poem starts thus:

> For loneliness and thought this is the hour:
> Now that thou smil'st so beautiful and bright,
> Oh! how I feel thy soul-subduing power,
> And gaze upon thy loveliness, sweet Nignt! (78)

Shelley's lines express the same infatuation with Night, but the style is far more concise, and the images are more vivid:

> Thou wovest dreams of joy and fear,
> Which make thee terrible and dear,—
>   Swift be thy flight:
> Wrap thy form in a mantle gray,
>   Star-inwrought!
>
> Blind with thine hair the eyes of Day;
> Kiss her until she be wearied out,
> Then wander o'er city, and sea, and land,
> Touching all with thine opiate wand—
>   Come, long-sought! (636-37)

Derozio adopted Byron's style and versification in his narrative poems. In several poems, he also adopted the metrical pattern of Byron's poetry. His use of tetrameter in "The Fakeer of Jungheera" is quite skilful:

> How like young spirits on the wing
> The viewless winds are wandering!
> Now o'er the flower-bells fair they creep
> Waking sweet odours out of sleep;
> Now stealing softly through the grass
> That rustles as the breezes pass,
> Just breathing such a gentle sigh
> As Love would live for ever by! (137)

Byron's poem "The Prisoner of Chillon" has the same metrical pattern and rhythmic beat:

> I heard the torrents leap and gush
> O'er channelled rock and broken bush;
> I saw the white-walled distant town,
> And whiter sails go skimming down.[17]

Kasiprasad Ghose was a versifier in English who trained himself in English rhyme and rhythm through arduous exercises. He himself writes: "I continued reading the best poets in a regular and measured tone which soon accustomed my ear to English rhythm."[18] Hence, his verses are accomplished ones with echoes from British poets. For example, lines from his poem published in *A Bengali Book of English Verse* bear resemblance to the metrical rhythm of the minor love poetry of the late Elizabethan age:

> I would I were the zephyr sweet,
> To kiss thy face and round it play;
> And when thou sigh'st for love, to greet
> Those sighs, and steal their sweetness away.[19]

The rhythm in the following lines from a poem "Love Me Or Not" by Thomas Campion is almost similar:

> Love me or not, love her I must or die;
> Leave me or not, follow her needs must I
> O that her grace would my wished comforts give.
> How rich in her, how happy should I live![20]

Apart from the metrical influence of the Elizabethan poetry, Kasiprasad Ghose often betrays the influence of the British Romantic poetry in his choice of imagery and outlook on life. "The Moon in September" offers a fine example of the influence of Romanticism. The objects of nature are presented as animate beings endowed with willpower:

> How like the breath of love the rustling breeze
> Is breathing through the fragrant sandal trees![21]

This tendency to imagine and represent inanimate things of nature as animate beings, as expressed in the following lines of the same poem more elaborately, is Shelleyan in character:

Like liquid silver yon soft-gliding stream
Wanders and glistens in the lunar beam,
Which like a modest maid, in love and fear
Shrinks, half-reluctant, from the clasp so dear
Of frequent-heaving waves. (94)

A typical example of Shelley's brilliant presentation of nature as an animate being is "Ode to the West Wind," where the poet imagines the West Wind as an animate being:

Thou who didst waken from his summer dreams
The blue Mediterranean, where she lay,
Lulled by the coil of his crystalline streams. (578)

Ghose's love of nature as displayed in various parts of his poetry also bears testimony to the Romantic influence. For example,

Where green-clad hills majestic stand,
    Where flowerets woo the scented gale;
Where Surya from his throne above
    With brightest colours paints the day;
Where ripplets rise to clasp their love,
Th' eluding beams that o'er them play.[22]

Rajnarain Dutt shows the influence of Walter Scott's ballads. The following lines from his poem "Song" bear the marks of the influence of Scott's ballads like "Lochinvar" both in rhythm and choice of subject:

The Beduins have mounted their steeds, and afar
Their cohorts advance in the proud ranks of war,
They have braced on the shield, and the sword by their side
And forth are they gone on a foray to ride.[23]

Lines from "Lochinvar" provide the inspiration:

O young Lochinvar is come out of the west,
Through all the wide Border his steed was the best,
And save his good broadsword he weapons had none,
He rode all unarmed, and he rode all alone.

So faithful in love, and so dauntless in war,
There never was Knight like the young Lochinvar.[24]

Under the influence of the Romantic poetry, Michael Madhusudan Dutt displays love of nature in the poetry of his early years, particularly in his untitled sonnets,

I saw young Zephyr pass from flower to flower,
While each, by turns, did softly bow its head,
And the fond pearly tears of rapture shed,
A sweet and tender welcome! Beauteous hour![25]

Again,

Beloved Lake, how oft I think of thee;
How oft I dream of thy calm silver breast,
Where moon-beams undisturbt ever rest,
And see themselves reflected beauteously—
Where no rude gales, with boisterous revelry,
Disturb the Lotus, thy sweet daughter coy;
But many a breeze, with perfumes gallantly
Comes to woo her, infusing purest Joy
To every heart. (453)

In his choice of octosyllabic metre in *The Captive Ladie*, Dutt follows Scott and Byron who popularised this metrical pattern in England. A few lines from *The Captive Ladie* will illustrate this:

There's light upon the heaving stream,
And music sweet as heard in dream,
And many a star upon its breast
Is calmly pillow'd unto rest,
While—there as on a silver throne—
All melancholy-veil'd—alone
Beneath the pale Moon's colder ray—
The Bride of him—the Lord of Day,
In silence droops—as in lone bow'r
The love-lorn maid at twilight hour! (481)

Byron's use of tetrameter in narrative poems like "The Prisoner of Chillon" seems to have provided a model for Dutt:

A small green isle, it seemed no more,
Scarcer broader thán my dungeon floor,
But in it there were three tall trees,
And o'er it blew the mountain breeze,
And by it there were waters flowing
And on it there were young flowers growing. (340)

Scott's use of tetrameter in narrative poems like "The Lay of the Last Minstrel" also seems to have inspired Dutt; a few lines from the poem may be quoted as illustration:

The way was long, the wind was cold,
The minstrel was infirm and old;
His withered cheek, and tresses grey,
Seemed to have known a better day;
The harp, his sole remaining joy,
Was carried by an orphan boy. (1)

The influence of Milton upon M.M. Dutt is considerably profound. Inspired by Milton, Dutt, for the first time in Bengali, wrote an epic in blank verse. In one of his English poems, "Visions of the Past," Dutt exhibits definite marks of Milton's influence. In this poem Dutt adopts the blank verse of Milton with some success:

Methought I saw those radiant beings that throng'd
Above—around—as if in guardianship,
Gaze on her while the beaming eloquence
Of admiration sat upon each brow
And wonderment—for utterance too deep! (472)

The influence of Milton is evident if a few lines from *Paradise Lost*, Book I are set beside the above-quoted lines of Dutt:

Of Man's first disobedience, and the fruit
Of that forbidden tree whose mortal taste
Brought death into the world, and all our woe,
With loss of Eden, till one greater man
Restore us, and regain the blissful seat.[26]

Dutt follows Milton's poetic method of evoking epic grandeur by the use of elaborate similes and descriptions in resonant lines: for example,

Oh!—didst thou wing me back to loveliest scenes
Primeval,—when creation brightly steep'd
In sunny glory smiled as the fair brow
Of Virgin pure—unclouded—when the blight
Of sin—like the vast shadow of some cloud
Darkwing'd and brooding o'er a sun-lit spot—
Dimm'd not the spring-ting'd beauty of her cheek. (472)

Dutt essayed his hand at sonnet-writing, in both Shakespearean and Petrarchan forms. He absorbed the influence of British poetry so much that it is markedly traceable even in his Bengali poetry.

Soshee Chunder Dutt, too, was influenced by Milton's blank verse. A few lines from *A Vision of Sumeru* bear testimony to this:

My dream is o'er; Sumeru's gods—
Sumeru's self hath past away,
By lightning blasted and by thunder unscath'd.
Within the deep Tartarean dell,
Perchance, yet tortured, unforgiven,
Unpitied, unreprieved, they rave and roar;
But in high heaven their ancient sway
They hold no more.[27]

Soshee Dutt's use of epithets like "adamantine," "ambrosial," "ethereal" and "Tartarean" recalls Milton's use of polysyllabic words in *Paradise Lost*.

C. Paul Verghese comments on the similarity between *A Vision of Sumeru* and *Paradise Lost*: "The Hindu gods and goddesses [in *A Vision of Sumeru*] awakened to the threat of their away on earth hold a council in Sumeru, the abode of Brahma, at his bidding, The council is a replica of the pandemonium in Milton's epic." (21)

Govin Chunder Dutt evinces an obvious influence of Keats. In his poem "A Farewell to Romance" Dutt clearly echoes Keats' "Ode to Autumn" in several lines. For example, the following lines from the poem,

Who hath not seen thee, fair one, when the day
Urges his coursers o'er the dappled clouds!
Flit o'er the dewsprent lawns in green array?[28]

imitate not only the sentence structure but also the manner of phrasing in Keats' "Ode to Autumn":

Who hath not seen thee oft amid thy store? (219)

Again the structural pattern of the following lines from Govin Dutt's poem,

Wherein thine image might be dimly spied,
While the winds dallied with thy bosom bare,
And raised thy robes; and oft in wantonness
Rippled thy mirror, to destroy thy dream?[29]

follow the structural pattern of lines from Keats' poem:

Where are the songs of spring? Ay, where are they?
Think not of them, thou hast thy music too—
While barred clouds bloom the soft-dying day,
And touch the stubble-plains with rosy hue. (219)

In the same poem Govin Dutt acknowledges the spell that the British poets cast upon him,

The varied melody of Shakespeare's shell,
The Doric flute of Milton, or the reed
Of 'sage and serious' Spenser ever dear,
Or what less deep, of late, thou lov'st to hear
The strains of Scott that stir the soul indeed. (23)

Hur Chunder Dutt imitates the jingling music and metrical pattern of Tennyson's "The Lady of Shalott" when he describes the eponymous heroine in the poem "Tarra Baee":

She sat upon her palfrey white,
That damsel fair and young,
And from the jewelled belt she wore,
Her trusty rapier hung;
And chieftains bold, and warriors proud,
Around her formed a gallant crowd. (25)

The similarity becomes obvious when the abovequoted lines are set beside the following lines from Tennyson's poem:

And from his blazoned baldric slung
A mighty silver bugle hung

And as he rode his armour rung,
Beside remote Shalott.[30]

Greece Chunder Dutt betrays the influence of the British Romantic poets in his description of Nature in several poems, as will be evident from a few lines from the poem "Sonnet: Near Nynee Thal":

How rich the prospect from this moss-grown seat!
The vineclad cottage in the warm recess
Shines like a palm tree of the wilderness,
When lone Arabia pants with torrid heat.
Below, where from the lake the hills retreat,
And the wild strawberry woos the Sun's caress,
How calm the cattle lie—how motionless!
Lulled by faint warblings from Deoban's feet,
How smooth the fields appear by yonder rill.[31]

Toru Dutt is a far more original poet than the other Bengali poets writing in English during the nineteenth century. She does not consciously imitate any poet but the influence of the British Romantic poets upon her is traceable in the several characteristics of her poetry.

In most of her poems Toru Dutt deals with the myths and legends of the past. Dutt's fondness for the past is definitely a feature of the British Romantic poets like Wordsworth, Coleridge, Byron, Shelley and Keats who have recurrently used themes from the classical and medieval past.

Dutt's frequent use of archaism in her poetry recalls the same tendency in Wordsworth, Scott and Burns.

Her description of nature in several parts of her mythological poems recalls the Romantic poets' love of Nature. For illustration, a few lines may be quoted,

Fair as a lotus when the moon
Kisses its opening petals red,
After sweet showers in sultry June![32]

These lines echo, however faintly, Shelley's comparisons in his poem "To a Skylark":

Like a glow-worm golden
In a dell of dew,
Scattering unbeholden
Its aerial hue

Among the flowers and grass which screen it from the view. (602)

Wordsworth's Lucy poems seem to have provided the inspiration to Dutt when she writes in "Buttoo":

All creatures and inanimate things
Shall be my tutors: I shall learn
From beast, and fish, and bird with wings
And rock, and stream, and trees and fern. (150)

The educative influence of nature as represented by Wordsworth in the Lucy poems and "Tintern Abbey" seems to have been accepted by Dutt when she writes the above lines.

The vision described by Dutt in "Jogadhya Uma" as in the following lines—

Sudden from out the water sprung
    A rounded arm, on which they saw
As high the lotus buds among
    It rose, the bracelet white, with awe.
Then a wide ripple tost and swung
    The blossoms on that liquid plain,
And lo! the arm so fair and young
    Sank in the waters down again.
They bowed before the mystic Power,
    And as they home returned in thought,
Each took from thence a lotus flower
    In memory of the day and spot (140)

recall Tennyson's lines in "Morte d'Arthur":

In those old days, one summer noon, an arm
Rose up from out the bosom of the lake,
Clothed in white samite, mystic, wonderful,
Holding the sword. (127)

The striking similarities point out that Toru Dutt was definitely influenced by the Romantic and Victorian poets both in her themes and style.

Manmohan Ghose went to England when he was seven years old. During his school and college days there, he imbibed the influence of the British poets so much so that his poetry seems to be an Englishman's poetry. George Sampson comments about Ghose's poetry: "a reader of his poems would readily take them as the work of an English poetic tradition."[33]

The influence of British poetry has affected several aspects of Ghose's poetry. While reviewing *Primavera*, a collection of poems to which Ghose contributed five poems, Oscar Wilde commented, "The temper of Keats, the moods of Matthew Arnold have influenced Mr. Ghose, and what better influences could a beginner have?"[34] The temper of Keats is apparent in Ghose's love of beauty, and the moods of Matthew Arnold are apparent in the sad strains that pervade Ghose's early poetry. The sentiments of Keats' "A thing of beauty is a joy for ever" is manifest in the lines from Ghose's poem "A Lament":

Birds fly with music in their wings;
And from the blue, rough sea
The fishes flash and leap;
There is a life of loveliest things
O'er thee, so fast asleep.[35]

The melancholy mood of Arnold is traceable in the lines from Ghose's poem "Raymond and Ida":

Heavy and low the sky is glooming:
Winter is coming! (2)

The following lines from "Raymond and Ida":

I cannot bear to see those tears:
Thy sad tones hurt my ear, (3)

recall, however faintly, D.G. Rossetti's lines in "The Blessed Damozel":

And laid her face between her hands
And wept. (I heard her tears.)[36]

Wordsworth seems to have exercised a deep influence on Ghose's poetry. The following lines from Ghose's poem "A Lament":

The roses on the hill
Are fragrant as before:
Only thy face, of all that's dear,
I shall see never more! (5)

remind us of lines from Wordsworth's Lucy poems, as quoted below:

'O mercy!' to myself I cried,
'If Lucy should be dead!' . . .
But she is in her grave, and, oh,
    The difference to me![37]

The Wordsworthian concept of the merging of the soul of the dead beloved with the beautiful objects of nature is found in several other poems by Ghose. The following quotations provide ample illustrations of the same:

Glowing she stands in the pure face of heaven,
In marriage with enchanted Nature given! (Poem VII, p.13)

O, she is gone? She never may return—
Past greenest leaves in Summer's heart to burn,
Past dew or flower or dreams or surges' lull,
To lie in deepest Nature beautiful. (Poem XIX, p. 36)

To one lovely face have passed forever
    Nature's own fair powers:
In her eyes the distant blue of heaven;
    On her cheek the flowers!. (Poem XXIX, p. 56)

The last quotation definitely echoes the idea contained in the following lines from Wordsworth's poem, "Three years she grew in sun and shower":

The floating clouds their state shall lend
'To her; for her the willow bend; . . .
And beauty born of murmuring sound
Shall pass into her face. (148)

There is often a note of escapism in Ghose's poetry which may be traced back to the escapist mood of Keats' "Ode to a Nightingale." The enchanting lines from Ghose's *Primavera*, Poem IV:

Deep-shaded will I lie, and deeper yet
    In night,where not a leaf its neighbour knows;
Forget the shining of the stars, forget

The vernal visitation of the rose;
And, far from all delights, prepare my heart's repose. (6)

and the lines from "Whispering Sleep":

Are not thy lips of honey, thy breath of honey-suckle,
Brother sweet of the breeze, wooing and whispering sleep?
Soft at our ears like a lover's thy vague lips tenderly murmur
"Kiss me!" they seem to say, "give me, poor heart, but a kiss." (24)

recall Keats' famous lines that chart the map of the poet's route of escape from the world of harsh reality:

Fade far away, dissolve, and quite forget . . .
Away! Away! for I will fly to thee . . .
But here there is no light,
Save what from heaven is with the breezes blown
Through verdurous glooms and winding mossy ways. (208)

The influence of Keats may be detected in Ghose's love of Greek names of myths. In the poem "To Stephen and May" Ghose expresses the romantic admiration of the Hellenic past:

He grieves me, tender, large and bright,
Hesperus in the western night;
And with sweet half-forgotten things
Zephyrus loads his western wings. (31)

About Ghose's Hellenic interests, Laurence Binyon commented: "He was well read in English poets, better read than I in Elizabethan and the older lyricists. But what struck me most was his enthusiastic appreciation of Greek poetry."[38]

Ghose exhibits the influence of Shelley, too. There is a poem by Ghose, entitled "The Indian Serenade," which recalls Shelley's famous poem of the same title. The last stanza of Ghose's poem, as quoted below:

Thou art not there! the night wind's breath
Sighs odorous through the Champak trees
The music of the tide beneath
Murmurs of love and quiet peace

And this my harp's goodnight to thee
O love beneath the Champak tree (38)

are definitely reminiscent of lines from Shelley's poem "The Indian Serenade":

The Champak odours fail
Like sweet thoughts in a dream. (580)

The two lines from Ghose's poem "The Lover and the Painter,"

'Twould ensphere!—
O intoxicated lover, let me hear (38)

echo the rhythm of the famous phrase in Shelley's poem "Ode to the West Wind":

. . . hear, oh, hear! (578)

V.K. Gokak comments: "Manmohan Ghose, Sri Aurobindo and Sarojini Naidu, who spent their impressionable years in England when the 'Decadent' poets dominated the scene, reveal the influence of this trend in their early poems. 'Decadence' became the main feature of Manmohan Ghose's poetry." (xx) A few lines, as quoted below, from the poetry of the Decadent poets like Lionel Johnson and Laurence Binyon show that Ghose's style has affinity with their style:

Through glades and glooms! And hails at last
The lovely scenes long past: long past.[39]

(Lionel Johnson, "Collins")

There is music in the midst of desolation
And a glory that shines upon our tears.[40]

(Laurence Binyon, "For the Fallen")

Besides the influence of British poets, Ghose's poetry embodies his love of England and English landscape. Laurence Binyon thought that England became for Ghose "a nursing-mother of imagination and the dear home of the Muses." (xvi) The general landscape presented in Ghose's early poetry is that of England where he lived up to the age of twentyfive. Specially, however, certain phrases and lines may be quoted where references to England are directly made. For example, in "London":

Farewell, sweetest country: out of my heart, you roses,
  Wayside roses, nodding, the slow traveller to keep.
 Too long have I drowsed alone in the meadows deep,
  Too long alone endured the silence nature espouses.
 Oh, the rush, the rapture of life! throngs, lights, houses,
  This is "London." I wake as a sentinel from sleep. (45)

The poem "The Garden Passion" begins with a description of nature which is sensuous and colourful, dreamy and romantic:

It is a garden, shy and sweet,
For youth and tongue-tied passion meet,
A green din garden shaded deep,
Breathing of lilies, love and sleep.
Here only flowers in darkness grow;
Here only whispering waters flow,
And fishes glide and linnets sing,
And summer dances with the spring. (58)

The tone and mood of the above description seem to owe, to a certain extent, to the tone and mood of Marvell's "Thoughts in a Garden" and Tennyson's "The Lotos-Eaters." The relevant stanzas from both the poems are quoted below:

What wondrous life in this I lead!
Ripe apples drop about my head;
The luscious clusters of the vine
Upon my mouth do crush their wine;
The nectarine and curious peach
Into my hands themselves do reach;
Stumbling on melons, as I pass,
Ensnared with flowers, I fall on grass.[41]

There is sweet music here that softer falls
Than petals from brown roses on the grass,
Or night-dews on still waters between walls
Of shadowy granite, in a gleaming pass; . . .
Here are cool mosses deep,
And through the moss the ivies creep,
And in the stream the long-leaved flowers weep,
And from the craggy ledge the poppy hangs in sleep. (102)

Manmohan Ghose's brother Aurobindo Ghose spent fourteen years in England and returned to India at the age of twenty-one after absorbing the influence of the British poets. Sri Aurobindo himself writes: "I dare say some influence of most of the great English poets and of others also, not English, can be traced in my poetry—I can myself see that of Milton, sometimes of Wordsworth and Arnold, but it was of the automatic kind—they came in unnoticed. I am not aware of much influence of Shelley and Coleridge, but since I read Shelley a great deal and took an intense pleasure in some of Coleridge's poetry, they may have been there without my knowledge. The one work of Keats that influenced me was *Hyperion*—I dare say my blank verse got something of his stamp through that."[42]

Two major influences on Sri Aurobindo's poetry are those of Keats and Milton. The sensuousness of Keats' imagery that is traceable in the imagery that Sri Aurobindo uses in his early poetry. "Songs to Myrtilla," one of Sri Aurobindo's earliest poems, bears the imprint of the influence of Keats' early poems like "I stood tip-toe upon a little hill," "Sleep and Poetry" and "Endymion." Lines like the following from "Songs to Myrtilla",

> Sweet is the night, sweet and cool
> As to parched lips a running pool;
> Sweet when the flowers have fallen asleep
> And only moonlit rivulets creep
> Like glow-worms in the dim and whispering wood,
> To commune with the quiet heart and solitude[43]

carry echoes from Keats' lines, as quoted below:

> I stood tip-toe upon a little hill
> The air was cooling, and so very still,
> That the sweet buds which with a modest pride
> Pull droopingly, in slanting curve aside,
> Their scantly leav'd, and finely tapering stems,
> Had not yet lost those starry diadems
> Caught from the early sobbing of the morn. (3)

The rhythm and mood of the following lines from Aurobindo's "Songs to Myrtilla,"

> And pleasant are her melodies,
> Rustle of winds, rustle of trees,

Birds' voices in the eaves,
Birds' voices in the green melodious leaves;
The herdsman's flute among his flocks,
Sweet water hurrying from reluctant rocks,
And all sweet hours and all sweet showers
And all sweet sounds that please the noonday flower (1)

bear resemblance to the rhythm and mood of the following lines from Keats' *Endymion*, Book I:

Such the sun, the moon,
Trees old, and young, sprouting a shady boon
For simple sheep; and such are daffodils
With the green world they live in; and clear rills
That for themselves a cooling covert make
'Gainst the hot season; the mid forest brake,
Rich with a sprinkling of their musk-rose blooms. (55)

The phrase "Too happy lover" and the repetition of the same in the following lines from "The Lover's Complaint" by Sri Aurobindo

Too happy lover, fill the lamp of bliss!
Too happy lover, drunk with Nisa's kiss! (20)

echo Keats' frequent use of the word "happy" in "Ode to a Nightingale" and "Ode on a Grecian Urn" respectively:

But being too happy in thine happiness, (207)

Ah, happy, happy boughs! . . .
More happy love! more happy, happy love! (210)

The influence of Keats' *Hyperion*, as has been acknowledged by Sri Aurobindo, is discernible in the blank verse of his longer poems like "Urvasie." The first few lines of the poem, characteristic of the whole composition, as quoted below,

Pururavus from Titah conflict ceased
Turned worldwards, through illimitable space
Had travelled like a star 'twixt earth and heaven
Slowly and brightly (189)

resemble the tone and rhythm of the blank verse used by Keats in *Hyperion*:

Deep in the shady sadness of a vale
Far sunken from the healthy breath of morn,
Far from the fiery noon, and eve's one star,
Sat gray-hair'd Saturn, quiet as a stone,
Still as the silence round about his lair;
Forest on forest hung about his head
Like cloud on cloud. (221)

"Khaled of the Sea" resembles Keats' *Lamia* both in its rhyming patterns and manner of description. The following lines from "Khaled of the Sea,"

Maiden, a marvellous bloom, a naked child;
All like a lily from her leaves escaped
The golden summer kissed her close and wrapped
In soft revealing sunshine—a sweet bareness,
A creature made of flowers and choicest fairness;
And all her limbs were like a luminous dream,
So wonderfully white they turn and gleam,
Her shoulder ivory richly bathed in gold,
Her sides a snowy wonder to behold,
Marble made amorous! her body fair
Seemed one with the divine, translucent air,
A light within the light, a glorious treasure,
A thing to hold, to press, to slay with pleasure (265)

follow the rhyming pattern and sensuousness of description as found in the lines from *Lamia*:

So done, upon the nymph his eyes he bent
Full of adoring tears and blandishment,
And towards her stept: she, like a moon in wane,
Faded before him, cower'd, nor could restrain
Her fearful sobs, self-folding like a flower
That faints into itself at evening hour:
But the God fostering her chilled hand,
She felt the warmth, her eyelids open'd bland,
And, like new flowers at morning song of bees,
Bloom'd, and gave up her honey to the lees
Into the green-recessed woods they flew;
Nor grew they pale, as mortal lovers do. (164)

Keats' method of concentrating romance in the following stanzas in "La Belle Dame Sans Merci,"

> I made a garland for her head,
> And bracelets too, and fragrant zone;
> She look'd at me as she did love,
> And made sweet moan.
>
> I set her on my pacing steed,
> And nothing else saw all day long;
> For sidelong would she bend, and sing
> A faery's song.
>
> She found me roots of relish sweet,
> And honey wild, and manna dew,
> And sure in language strange she said—
> 'I love thee true.'
>
> She took me to her elfin grot,
> And there she wept and sigh'd full sore,
> And there I shut her wild wild eyes
> With kisses four (350-51)

exercises an influence on Sri Aurobindo's method of description of the love-relation between the lover and the beloved in "Khaled of the Sea":

> For she, earth's wonder, hard to grasp as fire,
> She whom all ocean's secret depths admire,
> Laid her delicious cheek to his and flung
> Sweet, bare arms on his neck and round him clung:
> Her snowy side was of his being a part;
> Her naked breast burdened his throbbing heart,
> And all her hair streamed over him and the whiteness
> Of her was in his eyes and her soft brightness
> A joy beneath his hands to his embrace
> And he was clothed with her as in a dress . . .
>
> So rode they like a vision. all the time
> She murmured ascents as of linked rhyme
> Musical, in a language like the sea,
> Accents of undulating melody,
> For sometimes it was like a happy noon

Murmuring with waves and sometimes like the swoon
Of calm, a silence heard, or rich by noise
Of rivers pouring with their seaward voice
And leaping laughter and sometimes was wild
And passionate as the sobbing of a child. (269-70)

While Keats is concise and suggestive, Sri Aurobindo is elaborate and picturesque. But the resemblances between the two poets in the exploration of the motif of romance are often striking, and indicate the influence of the former poet upon the latter.

On his own admission, Sri Aurobindo imbibed the influence of Milton's poetic manner. Miltonic influence is traceable in Sri Aurobindo's use of blank verse, epic similes, high-sounding proper nouns, involved constructions and inversions in his longer narrative poems.

Sri Aurobindo has used blank verse in the four cantos of "Urvasie," and the long poems "Love and Death," "Khaled of the Sea," "Baji Prabhou," "Chitranagada," "Ulopie" and "The Tale of Nala." In writing the blank verse, as in the following lines from "Baji Prabhou."

A noon of Deccan with its tyrant glare
Oppressed the earth; the hills stood deep in haze,
And sweltering athirst the fields glared up
Longing for water in the courses parched
Of streams long dead. Nature and man alike,
Imprisoned by a bronze and brilliant sky,
Sought an escape from that wide trance of heat. (281)

Sri Aurobindo might have in mind the sonority and resonance of Milton's blank verse as illustrated in the lines from *Paradise Lost*, Book IV:

O for that warning voice, which he who saw
Th' Apocalypse, heard cry in heav'n aloud,
Then when the Dragon, put to second rout,
Came furious down to be reveng'd on men,
We to th' inhabitants on Earth! (73)

Milton's successful aptitude for developing an elaborate simile for a vivid portrayal of a scene, as found in his description of Satan's large army in *Paradise Lost*, Book I,

As Bees
In spring time, when the Sun with Taurus rides,
Pour thir populous youth about the Hive
In clusters; they among fresh dews and flowers
Flie to and fro, or on the smoothed Plank,
The suburb of thir straw-built citadel,
New rub'd with Baume, expatiate and confer
Their state affairs. So thick the aerie crowd
Swarmd and were strait'nd (25)

exercises an influence upon Sri Aurobindo who developed an elaborate simile to invoke a scene vividly along with its orchestration of sensations, as in the following lines from "Love and Death":

As a bright bird comes flying
From airy extravagance to his own home,
And breasts his mate, and feels her all his goal,
So from boon sunlight and the fresh chill wave
Which swirled and lapped between the slumbering fields,
From forest pools and wanderings mid leaves
Through emerald ever-new discoveries,
Mysterious hillsides ranged and buoyant-swift
Races with our wild brothers in the meads,
Came Ruru back to the white-bosomed girl,
Strong-winged to pleasure. (232)

The use of a string of proper names for musical effects, as in the lines from "Urvasie,"

So danced they numberless as dew-drops gleam,
Menaca, Misracayshie, Mullica,
Rumbha, Nelabha, Shela, Nolinie,
Lolita, Lavonya and Tilottama,—
Many delightful names; among them she (190)

may be traced back to Milton who was fond of juxtaposing resonant nouns for musical effects, as in the following lines from *Paradise Lost*, Book IX:

. . . all thir known vertue appears
Productive in Herb, Plant, and nobler birth
Of Creatures animate with gradual life

Of Growth, Sense, Reason, all summed up in Man.
. . . sweet interchange
Of Hill and Vallie, Rivers, Woods and Plaines,
Now Land, now Sea, and Shores with Forest crown'd,
Rocks, Dens, and Caves. (185)

Involved constructions and inversions are found galore in Sri Aurobindo. One small example from "Urvasie" is quoted below:

He
By beauty and strength incomparable shall rule. (217)

This tendency of Sri Aurobindo may be considered an outcome of his close study of Milton who made himself an expert in the use of involved constructions and inversions of style as in the following lines from *Paradise Lost*, Book X:

So spake our Father penitent, nor Eve
Felt less remorse; they forthwith to the place
Repairing where he judg'd them prostrate fell
Before him reverent. (241)

Sri Aurobindo was so much influenced by Milton that one can trace in Sri Aurobindo's long narrative poems in blank verse even minute details of Milton's style.

Since Swami Vivekananda did not follow any formal pattern or fixed literary style, and his poetry was more an expression of his spirituality than a pure literary endeavour, his English poetry does not betray clearly the influence of any particular British poet.

On the whole, however, the above analysis demonstrates that the English poetry written by Bengalis during the nineteenth century bears the definite stamp of the influence of British poetry. The Bengalis writing poetry in English during that period learnt their craft from the British poets. No wonder, then, that though the nineteenth-century English poetry of Bengal originated in Bengal, and embodied to the ideas and imagination of the Bengalis, this poetry could not escape the shaping influence of British poetry. The impact of English education in the nineteenth-century Bengal resulted in the beginning and growth of English poetry by Bengalis.

II.

The influence of Christianity in the nineteenth-century English poetry of Bengal is first discernible in the poetry of Michael Madhusudan Dutt who embraced Christianity on 9 February 1843. The hymn sung on the occasion by the congregation was composed by Madhusudan Dutt himself; and he assumed the Christian name Michael. The whole hymn is quoted below:

Long sunk in Superstition's night,
By sin and Satan driven—
I saw not,—cared not for the light
That leads the blind to Heaven.

I sat in darkness,—Reason's eye
Was shut,—was closed in me;
I hasten'd to Eternity
O'er Error's dreadful sea!

But now, at length thy grace, o Lord!
Bids all around me shine:
I drink thy sweet,—thy precious word,
I kneel before thy shrine!—

I've broken Affection's tenderest ties
For my blest Savior's sake:-
All, all I love beneath the skies,
Lord! I for thee forsake! (467)

Though Derozio, the first Indian poet to write poetry in English, was a Christian, he did not compose any poem in praise of Christ and Christianity. It is M.M. Dutt who, amongst the Indian poets writing in English, first composed poetry to express the westernized Indians' eager desire to liberate themselves from the superstitions of the Hindu society by embracing Christianity. Amalendu Bose remarks: "The reason for Madhusudan's embracement of Christianity was his firm conviction that, for India and Indians of his day, the road to civilization lay through Christianization and Europeanization, that it was primarily through Christianity that an Indian could hope to be liberated from the stifling stranglehold of a thousand and one superstitions."[44]

The other poem, where M.M. Dutt writes about Christ and Christianity, is *Visions of the Past*. C.Paul Verghese comments: "His *Visions of the Past* is an assertion of his faith in Christianity." (19) John B. Alphonso-Karkala makes an analysis of the thematic and structural pattern of the poem: "These 'visions' deal with Christian themes: primeval innocence, the temptation of man, his fall, and his redemption." (49)

The poem was published in fragments; but it leaves an unfailing impression of the poet's firm conviction regarding the grace bestowed upon the erring humanity by the Son of God who himself repented on behalf of it. The introductory sonnet ends on that note of faith:

> I wept!—A Prodigal once weeping sought,
> His Father's breast,—and found love unforgot! (470)

This sentiment runs through the following lines which image forth Christ on the Cross:

> I look'd—the sun had veil'd his dazzling brow—
> As when he saw upon thee, Calvarie!
> The Pilgrim from His Father's bosom—He—
> His God—with blood-stain'd brow and crown of thorn
> Die on th' accursed tree—yen—die to save—
> And dying pray for those who shed His blood! (475)

Amalendu Bose pertinently remarks: "This brief portrait of Christ on the cross, a crown of thorns on his head, shows that though Michael does not seem to have spoken much of his religious faith, the concept of Jesus, undergoing the ultimate suffering on behalf of all mankind, was a matter of deep-seated conviction with him." (30)

M.M. Dutt's absorption of the teachings of Christ and understanding of the Christian faith are manifest in the concluding lines of the poem:

> They wept—but not in dark despair—they wept
> As Guilt—all penitent—when, Mercy! thou
> Dost plead—nor plead in vain—in gentle strains
> To justice stern to win redeeming grace! (478)

Soshee Chunder Dutt's *A Vision of Sumeru* (1878) follows M.M. Dutt's *Vision of the Past* in asserting faith in Christianity. In this poem the poet calls Brahma, Vishnu and Shiva "false Indian deities,"[45] and depicts the triumph of the worship of Jesus.

Greece Chunder Dutt was responsible for the conversion of the whole Dutt family to Christianity. His book, *Cherry Blossoms* (1887), contains poems on the Revelation of St. John the Divine. His poetry often uses Christian imagery. For example:

> . . . I love to hear
> My true love read, in assents silvery clear,
> Of Jesus musing by the desert well.[46]

The poets of the *Dutt Family Album* (1870) were converts to Christianity: their poetry exhibits an unusual reverence for Christian themes. This is explicit in Govin Chunder Dutt's poem addressed to his wife:

> Wilt thou too join the scoffing crowd,
> The cold, the heartless, and the proud,
> Who curse the hallowed morn
> When, daring idols to disown,
> I knelt before the Saviour's throne?[47]

However, the love of Christianity as evidenced in the poems composed by some of the nineteenth-century Bengali poets writing in English is a part of the social scene in Bengal during the Renaissance period. Hence we safely regard it as a by-product of the historical phenomenon. However, what is remarkable is that this phenomenon left its deep impress upon the nineteenth-century English poetry of Bengal.

NOTES

1. R.C. Majumdar, *Renascent India* (Calcutta, 1976), p. 175.
2. R.C. Majumdar, *Freedom Movement of India* (Calcutta, 1971), Vol. I, p. 272.
3. K.M. Munshi, *Rabindranath and Indian Renaissance*, an address delivered at Santiniketan on August 9, 1961.
4. H.M. Williams, *Indo-Anglian Literature* (Madras, 1976), p. 15.
5. V.K. Gokak, ed., Introduction, *The Golden Treasury of Indo-Anglian Poetry* (New Delhi, 1978), p. xix.
6. M.K. Naik, "Echo and Voice in Indian Poetry in English," *Indian Response to English Poetry*, ed. by M.K. Naik et al (Madras, 1970), p. 270.
7. K.R. Srinivasa Iyengar, *Indian Writing in English* (New Delhi, 1983), p. 35.

8. A.N. Dwivedi, ed., Introduction, *Indian Poetry in English* (New Delhi, 1980), p. 16.
9. M.K. Naik, *A History of Indian English Literature* (New Delhi, 1982), p. 23.
10. John B. Alphonso-Karkala, *Indo-English Literature in the Nineteenth Century* (Mysore, 1970), p. 23.
11. C. Paul Verghese, *Problems of the Indian Creative Writer in English* (Bombay, 1971), p. 10.
12. Susobhan Sarkar, Introduction, *Derozio*: *Poems*, selected by P. Lal (Calcutta, 1972), p. ii
13. E.W. Madge, *Henry Derozio*: *the Eurasian Poet and Reformer*, ed. Subir Ray Choudhuri (Calcutta, 1967), p. 23.
14. H.L.V. Derozio, *Poems*, ed. by F.B. Bradley-Birt (Calcutta, 1980), p. 1.
15. John Keats, *The Poetical Works* (London, 1959), p. 350.
16. P.B. Shelley, *The Complete Poetical Works* (London, 1960), p. 580.
17. Lord Byron, *The Poetical Works* (London, 1970), p. 340.
18 Qtd. Lotika Basu, *Indian Writers of English Verse* (Calcutta, 1933), p. 19.
19. T.O.D. Dunn, ed., *A Bengali Book of English Verse* (London, 1918), p. 75.
20. W. Peacock, ed., *English Verse* (London, 1971), Vol. II. p. 2.
21. K.C. Lahiri, ed., *Indo-English Poetry in Bengal* (Calcutta, 1974), p. 24.
22. V.K. Gokak, p. 7.
23. *Ibid.*, p. 10.
24. Walter Scott, *The Poetical Works* (London, 1971), p. 142.
25. *Madhusudan Rachanavali*, ed. Khetra Gupta (Calcutta, 1982), p. 452.
26. John Milton, *The Poetical Works* (London, 1958), p. 5.
27. Qtd. C. Paul Verthese, *Indian Creative Writer in English*, p. 21.
28. V.K. Gokak, p. 21.
29. *Ibid.*, p. 22.
30. Lord Tennyson, *The Poems and Plays* (New York, 1938), p. 55.
31. K.C. Lahiri, p. 34.
32. Toru Dutt, *Ancient Ballads and Legends of Hindustan*, ed. A.N. Dwivedi (Bareilly, 1976), p. 109.
33. George Sampson, *The Concise Cambridge History of English Literature* (Cambridge, 1941), p. 914.
34. Oscar Wilde, *Reviews* (London, 1908), pp. 546-47.
35. Manmohan Ghose, *Collected Poems* (Calcutta, 1970), Vol. I, p. 5.
36. D.G. Rossetti, *Poems and Translations* (London, 1959), p. 5.
37. William Wordsworth, *Poetical Works* (London, 1959), p. 86.
38. Qtd. John B. Alphonso-Karkala, p. 58.
39. W. Peacock, ed., *English Verse* (London, 1969), Vol. V, p. 520.
40. F.T. Palgrave, ed., *The Golden Treasury* (London, 1963), p. 493.
41. Andrew Marvell, *Poems* (London, 1964), p. 75.
42. Sri Aurobindo, *On Himself*, Centenary Volume (Pondicherry, 1972), Vol. 26, p. 267.

43. Sri Aurobindo, *Collected Poems* (Pondicherry, 1972), p. 1.
44. Amalendu Bose, *Michael Madhusudan Dutt* (New Delhi, 1981), p. 24.
45. C. Paul Verghese, p. 20.
46. *Ibid.*, p. 22.
47. Padmini Sen Gupta, *Toru Dutt* (New Delhi, 1977), p. 20.

Social Reforms

In the preceding chapter I have shown that the nineteenth-century English poetry of Bengal reflects the influence of English education and culture. The absorption of the Western influence acted as a liberating force and the Bengalis of the Renaissance period exhibited a reformistic zeal that swept over the whole province.

Derozio takes the lead role in this respect. V.K. Gokak remarks: "The championing of the Indian widow starts with Derozio."[1] C. Paul Verghese comments: "Derozio's ardour for social reform shows itself in this poem *The Fakir of Jungheera*."[2] John B. Alphonso-Karkala points out the reformistic element: "In his longer work *The Fakir of Jungheera* (1828) Henry Derozio attempts to tell a long tale . . . exposing the social evil of *Sati*."[3]

The Fakeer of Jungheera is a long poem alternating between description and comment, both vivid, poignant and full of significance. The first nine sections of the poem present through a series of evocative images the picture of the young woman taken along in a procession accompanied by horses and trumpeteers to the altar of a pyre where she will be burnt to ashes, according to the custom of the *sati*. The chorus of the ladies and brahmins leading the procession, however, present an idealized picture of the *sati*:

Chorus of Women

Happy! thrice happy! thy lord shall there meet thee,
    Twined round his heart shalt thou ever remain,
Happy! bright angels are longing to greet thee,
    Tuned are their harp-strings, and ready their strain.
On to the altar, and scatter the flower,
    Sweeten the path as ye wander along;
On to the altar! another blest hour.
    Bring to her spirit the kinnura's song.[4]

Chorus of Brahmins

Bring the balm, and bring the myrrh,
Sweet as is the breath of her
Who upon the funeral pyre
Shall, ere Surya sets, expire. (145)

In Section X, Derozio exposes the hypocrisy of the brahmins and the women, and satirises the social custom of the *sati*. He sharpens his satire in order to express his aversion from the inhuman superstitious custom that slays human beings in the name of a religious practice:

O! this is but the world's unfeeling way
To goad the victim that it soon will slay,
And like a demon 'tis its custom still
To laugh at sorrow, and then coldly kill. (147)

Though the poem is a narrative tale of romance and adventure, the poet inserts in the same his criticism of the evils of superstitious social customs. Thus the satire becomes a part and parcel of the narrative framework.

The satire is counterpointed by the poet's appreciation of the woman's independence in matters of choice which is suppressed under the social customs of the time. The poet describes the authority who imposes these customs as "mean" and "cruel." (150) Since Nuleeni, the heroine, loves a person other than her husband, the poet does not approve of the torture that the Brahmins inflict on her to self-immolation on the funeral pyre of her husband. The poet raises the question:

. . . could she be,
While by her husband's lifeless form, unmoved
If ever she that lifeless form had loved? (152)

And he warns the readers and perhaps all the people of the time that they should not tyrannize over the womankind through misjudgement and misrepresentation: "Of woman judge not thus." (152)

The poet's profound sympathy with the women persecuted under the tyrannous social customs finds expression time and again throughout the poem:

Alas! that woman e'er should be
Bowed to the earth with misery,

And that her soul from pleasure's sky
Should like a meteor fall from high! . . .
But ah! most sad when woman gay
Must swan-like sing her dying lay! (153-54)

Derozio's protest against the inhuman social customs is voiced directly in *The Fakeer of Jungheera*. E.F. Oaten comments on the "real yet manly pathos, imaginative thought and musical and appropriate diction"[5] with which the poet depicts the inhumanity of *sati*, the false morality of the women and the hypocritical chanting of the Brahmins. John B. Alphonso-Karkala rightly points out: "What is more important in his poem is his theme—his attempt to expose the social evils of a decadent society with greater subtlety than Raja Rammohan Roy's outright denunciation." (42)

Derozio portrays the gruesome performance of the *sati* with a profound note of pathos and irony in section XXI:

Full soon the link of being's chain
That holds Nuleeni yet below,
Shall be for ever snapped in twain—
And then adieu to mortal woe!
Before the pile she bends her brow,
With all affections she must part,
And those that cling to earth must now
At once be severed from her heart.—
And from her head the wreath she takes,
Seven circuits round the pile she makes,
And now with baleful brand on fire
She slowly mounts the dreadful pyre! (161)

From Section XXII of Canto I to Section XVI of Canto 2 of the poem, Derozio paints an idyllic scene of love and romance between Nuleeni and her robber-lover who rescues her from the immolation on the pyre. The poet portrays the love between the heroine and her lover in a very romantic manner: the poet espouses the love, which is born of free choice, between Nuleeni and the robber-lover—this fact emphasizes Derozio's castigation of the obnoxious social custom that robs a woman of her choice and subjugates her to the ignominious practice of *sati*. However, it should also be noted that the poet's reformistic zeal has not turned his poetry into mere tract. The poetic merit of the poem is not diminished; rather the worth of the poem is heightened by the poet's sympathy for the oppressed and the downtrodden.

The remaining sections of Canto 2 depict in detail the fight between the robber-lover and Nuleeni's father who ultimately vanquishes the opponent. Nuleeni commits suicide as soon as her lover dies. By sympathising with Nuleeni who has chosen her course of action according to the dictates of her conscience, perception and reasoning, Derozio has championed the cause of woman's freedom from the thraldom of social customs. In ultimate analysis, *The Fakeer of Jungheera* appears to be the embodiment of the poet's ideal of the emancipated woman. R.K. Dasgupta calls him "the first evangelist of free thought in the traditional society of early nineteenth century Bengal."

Kasiprasad Ghose draws a stirring picture of a bereaved young Hindu woman who suffers the pain and privation of long widowhood as she is not permitted by the Hindu society to marry again. The social custom made it a frequent practice among the Hindus to get their young girls married to an aged man who expires within a few years of marriage to leave his wife a widow at an early age. The title of the poem is "To a Young Hindu Widow." The poet compares the widow to a desert flower:

> Ah, fair one! lone as desert flower,
> Where bloom and beauty are in vain:
> How dark was that too fatal hour
> Which brought thee lasting grief and pain![6]

The poet shows himself a true reformer in spirit and temperament when he asks the rhetorical question,

> And is there none—O! can it be?
> None warm or friendly in thy cause?
> Has pitiless humanity
> Forgot its sacred ties and laws? (5)

Ghose sympathises with the widow and expresses regret for her lot when he concludes the poem with a question to which there can be only one appalling answer in the existing social set-up:

> Is this the all, or should it be
> The all that here to thee is left?
> And must the world remain to thee
> A scene of every charm bereft? (6)

Thus the English poetry of Bengal during the nineteenth century records protest and pathos when and where injustice is perpetrated by the autocrats of the superstitious social system.

Though Michael Madhusudan Dutt was a Westernized Indian, he hardly expressed any ardour for social reforms in his English poetry. Only in the poem or hymn which was composed by him on the occasion of his baptismal, he expressed his impatience with the superstitious customs of his society. In that poem, quoted in the last chapter, the poet celebrates his conversion to Christianity as a mode of liberation from the superstitions of his Hindu society "long sunk in superstition's night."

One of the contributors to the *Dutt Family Album* (1870), Omesh Chunder Dutt hints at the narrow attitude of the then Hindu society towards women, and how the malefolk keep the wives in confinement in the name of chastity. In the poem entitled "The Hindu Wife to her Husband," the poet, in the guise of the wife, depicts the narrow confinement to which the woman as *purdanashin* is subjected:

> From pleasures of this life debarred,
> They tell me that my lot is hard,
> That, forc'd like prison'd bird to pine,
> Such joys as theirs can ne'er be mine;
> That beauty, wit and gems are vain
> If hidden they must thus remain.[7]

From a study of the above poems, it seems that, of all the superstitions and allied malpractices, the Bengali poets writing in English during the nineteenth century focussed attention mainly on the problems of women in the Hindu society.

NOTES

1. V.K. Gokak, ed., *The Golden Treasury of Indo-Anglian Poetry* (New Delhi, 1978), p. xxiii.
2. C. Paul Verghese, *Problems of the Indian Creative Writer in English* (Bombay, 1971), p. 7.
3. John B. Alphonso-Karkala, *Indo-English Literature in the Nineteenth Century* (Mysore, 1970), p. 41.
4. Derozio, *Poems*, ed. F.B. Bradley-Birt (Calcutta, 1980), p. 144.
5. E.F. Oaten, *A Sketch of Anglo-Indian Literature* (London, 1908), p. 7.
6. V.K. Gokak, p. 5.
7. K.C. Lahiri, ed., *Indo-English Poetry in Bengal* (Calcutta, 1974), p. 67.

The Glory That was India

After the introduction of English education, Bengalis came under the influence of English literature. How the Bengali poets writing in English imbibed the influence of English literature has been traced earlier. The Western influence changed their attitude towards the age-old Bengali customs which appeared to them as mere superstitions. Their attempt to voice their contempt of superstitious customs has also been discussed. They advocated several social reforms through their poetry. Along with their reformistic zeal, they showed a deep interest in the pure and pristine culture of ancient India which lay hidden so long under the veil of ignorance. These poets chose, for poetic treatment, themes from the glorious past of India. In this chapter, this aspect of the nineteenth-century English poetry of Bengal will be dealt with.

Though a European by birth, Derozio remained loyal and true to the spirit of the Bengal Renaissance while paying rich tributes to the glorious past of India. His intense awareness of the greatness of India's past is manifest in most of his poems. "The Harp of India" recalls the glory of the past of India through an image of the musical instrument which produced sweet sounds once upon a time but is totally silent now:

> Thy music once was sweet.[1]

The glory is set off by the present condition of decay:

> Neglected, mute, and desolate art thou. (1)

"To India—My Native Land" expresses the poet's admiration of India's past more lucidly. The first two lines of the poem present a vivid image of ancient India with all her glory:

> My country! in thy day of glory past
> A beauteous halo circled round thy brow. (2)

The poet goes to the extent of imagining India as a goddess because of the halo of her glory:

> And worshipped as a deity thou wast. (2)

Derozio is so confident about the greatness of India's past that he desires to review and recollect the same with passionate devotion:

> Well—let me dive into the depths of time,
> And bring from out the ages that have rolled
> A few small fragments of those wrecks sublime. (2)

The sublime past provides a marked contrast to the decadent and stagnant conditions of the present. The awareness of this contrast leads the poet to a sad lament:

> Where is that glory, where that reverence now? (2)

M.K. Naik points out: "Derozio is a pioneer in the use of Indian myth and legend, imagery and diction." (23) Pallav Sengupta remarks on the influence of the *Vedas* in the "Hymn to the Sun" which forms a part of *The Fakeer of Jungheera*. He quotes Derozio's own note on the poem: "The Vedas, which are supposed to contain the essence of wisdom, declare in various places, wherever language of praise is employed the object of such praise is the Deity or Brihm. Thus fire is Brihm, the sun is Brihm. . . . It is necessary to state that all prayers in the ceremony of female immolation are addressed to the sun."[2] The following lines from the poem exemplify the Vedic influence:

> God of this beauteous world! whom earth and heaven
>   Adore in concert and in concert love,
> Whose praise is hymned by the eternal seven
>   Bright whirling minstrels of the court above.
> God of this glorious universe!—the sea
>   Smiles in thy glance, and gladdens in thy ray;
> And lifted up its voice in praise to thee
>   Giver of good, creator of day. (157-58)

That Derozio adopted the Vedic prayer to the sun in his poem is a clear indication of this admiration of India's ancient glory as enshrined in her scriptures.

The next poet to sing of the past glory of India is Gooroo Churn Dutt who in his poem "Introductory Lines" refers repeatedly to the contrast between the past glory and the present degradation:

> If then amongst thy sons a fallen race,
> Alas! degraded low, (unhappy days!)[3]

The "fallen" state of India reminds the poet of "thy mysterious shastras' lore" and "the fire of any ancient stage."

Michael Madhusudan Dutt became famous as a Bengali poet who transformed an episode from the *Ramayana* into an epic. In his English poetry, too, Dutt makes use of Indian legend, myth and stories from ancient Indian history. H.M. Williams rightly remarks: "*The Captive Ladie* (1849) is a narrative poem on a subject taken from Indian history interspersed with references to Hindu myths and legends."[4]

C. Paul Verghese also points out that the content of the poem is derived from the past history of India: "*The Captive Ladie* is Indian insofar as the poet makes a conscious effort to use Indian imagery, and expresses Indian sentiments and tells an Indian story."[5] Dutt harks back to the past, and revives a part of Indian history in his long poem. It is the story of the King of Delhi who after winning his bride forcibly from her father, the King of Kanauj, is threatened by the conquering Mohamed of Ghazni. He is refused aid by the King of Kanauj and then he and his "captive ladie" commit suicide by throwing themselves on a funeral pyre.

Indian mythology is invoked in several parts of the poem. The minstrel, who is the narrator of the poem, refers to the story of Rama and Sita and that of Kauravas and Pandavas. There is also the mention of Kali the goddess and Shiva the god who appear in a dream to Baiza the bride. These references to the stories from Indian mythology contribute to the evocation of the special ethos and milieu of the poem.

The reference to Krishna with his flute and the maidens around him in the following lines creates an atmosphere, imbued with the memory of the legendary past of India:

> How fondly in the moon-lit bow'r,
> When mid-night came with star and flow'r,
> Young Krishna with his maidens fair
> Rov'd joyously and sported there—
> Or, on the Jumna's holy stream
> Where star-light came to sleep and dream,
> From his light skiff, that sped along,

His soft reed breath'd the gayest song,
Which swelling on the fitful sweep
Of the lone night-wind's sigh—so deep—
Wing'd ravishment where'er it fell—
Love's accents in their aery spell![6]

In this context, John B. Alphonso-Karkala's comment is quite pertinent: "He [Dutt] embellished his English verse [in *Captive Ladie*], at times by literally translating Sanskrit descriptive phrases, such as 'the bride of him—the lord of Day [sun]' to suggest a water lily; at other times, by making allusions to persons, or places, or incidents in the *Ramayana* or the *Mahabharata* or the *Puranas*"[7] Some of the allusions may be adduced here. For example, a part of the poem is called "The Feast of Victory"; the poet himself elaborates on the implications of the Feast: "the 'Feast of Victory'—or, as it is called in Sanscrit the 'Raj Shooio Jugum' is described at great length in the Second Book of the far-famed 'Mohabharut'." (509)

Dutt refers to the stories from the *Puranas* like *Chandni* in the following lines:

Where there the bard in loftier strain,
Sang war and mighty heroes slain—
How when Nesumba's impious pride
Swell'd high like stormlash'd ocean tide,
And made his very Mother Earth
Oft curse the hour she gave him birth. (487)

Dutt himself adds footnotes on his own borrowing of ideas and images from the *Puranas*.

A few lines later Dutt makes use of the image of Sita being abducted by Ravana:

Or—how to Beauty's lonely bow'r
The false one came at noon-tide hour,
And pluckt its brightest-fairest flow'r. (487)

The poet refers to scenes from the *Mahabharata* as in the following lines:

Or—how like the sunny tide
Of ocean rolling far and wide,
The Guru came in all his pride. (488)

The pictures from the ancient legends and mythology of India produce a cumulative effect. They pinpoint the fact that the Bengali poets writing in English during the nineteenth century loved to recreate scenes from India's past. Thus they showed a keen interest in re-discovering the past of their own country, and by invoking the past of India in their poetry they familiarized the readers with the same.

In Canto II of the poem Dutt carries on the method of incorporating frequent references to the Indian mythology in the framework of the narrative. The poet chose Husteena as the locale of the narrative because of its mythological associations; he himself notes: "Husteena was the birth-place of the Pandu and Kuru princes of war-like notoriety." (510) The poet evokes the grandeur of Husteena of the *Mahabharata*:

But must she fall,—that city fair,
Who sits her like an empress there—
The tow'r-tiara'd bride of Time—
The brightest of her sunny clime—
Mother of heroes once whose name,
Like thunder-winged whirl-winds came,
And shook the mightiest thrones below,
And pal'd the brow of proudest foe? (497)

The gods and goddesses of Hindu religion are described in several parts of Canto II with enough accuracy to inspire awe and aura associated with those deities. For example, the goddess Kali is represented in the dream of Baiza thus:

Methought there came a warrior-maid,
With blood-stained brow and sheathless blade;
Dark was her hue, as darkest cloud,
Which comes the Moon's fair face to shroud,—
And 'round her waist a hideous zone,
Of hands with charnel lightnings shone,
And long the garland which she wore,
Of heads all bath'd in streaming gore,
How fierce the eyes by death unseal'd
And blasting gleams which they reveal'd!
I shudder'd—tho' I knew 'twas she,
The awful, ruthless Deity,
On whose dread altar like a flood,
There flows for aye her victim's blood! (500-1)

The description of Kali is followed by the description of Shiva:

> I wept—when, lo!—before me stood—
> One girt with snakes of flow'r-crown'd hood,—
> Tall as the loftiest palm that be,
> Beneath you heaven's blue canopy!—
> His hue was pale,—and wild his eyes,
> Roll'd bright like meteors of the skies,
> A fiery trident high he bore,—
> Methought, it, too, was bath'd in gore. (501)

Dutt includes a reference to Ganga in the description of Shiva:

> And from his golden crown aloft,—
> There came still murmurs sweet and soft,
> Like the low plaints of some young rill,
> When check'd its thoughtless, wandering will! (501)

Dutt evokes the image of Lakshmi in these lines:

> I look'd—there stood beside my bed,
> A child of Light—a heavenly maid!—
> Upon her brow a diadem,
> Glisten'd with many a starry gem;
> But the calm lustre of her eye,
> Methought aye pal'd their radiancy,—
> And dewy wreaths of flowers that be,
> From realms of Immortality,
> Encircling bloom'd—all beauteously!
> A moon-lit halo around her shone,
> Like dreams of joy link'd 'round Love's throne,
> And sweet the aery Symphony,
> From viewless harps came sweeping by! (501-2)

Dutt's lines are instinct with awe and reverence that lend a tone of sublimity to the poem. Apart from contributing to the tonal effect of the poem, the description of the deities forms an integral part of the narrative, as the three deities, Kali, Shiva and Lakshmi, as pointed out by Dutt himself, "are supposed to be the guardian deities of royal families." (511)

In the poem, "King Porus," Dutt presents a heroic figure from the ancient history of India. King Porus was a valiant Indian king. Emperor

Alexander of Greece was so impressed by the bravery and heroism of King Porus that the former released the latter and restored the kingdom to him. The poet pays rich tributes to King Porus for his heroism and bravery:

> But, Ind! thy unsuspecting sons
> Did heedless slumber,—while the foe
> Came in stealthy step of death,—
> Came as the tiger, noiseless, slow,
> To close at once its victim's breath!
> Alas' they knew not 'midst this gloom,
> This war of elements, was nurst,—
> Like to an earthquake in the womb
> Of a volcano,—deep and low—
> A deadlier storm—on them to burst! (464)

Towards the end of the poem Dutt puts in verse the heroic sage of King Porus not bowing down before Alexander but maintaining his heroic uprightness with a brave front:

> While 'round Earth's mightiest monarchs bow'd:
> He couched not as a slave—
> He stooped not—bent not there his knee,—
> But stood—as stands an oak.
> Unbent—in native majesty!
> 'How should I treat thee?' ask'd
> The mighty king of Macedon,—
> 'Aye—as a king!' respons'd
> In royal pride Ind's haughty son:
> The king was pleased,
> And him released.
> Thus India's crown was lost and won. (466)

In the poem "King Porus," Dutt recaptures a glorious event of heroism and bravery from the past history of India. By such poetic recollection of the past of India, Dutt, like the other nineteenth-century Bengali poets writing in English, inspired the Indians of the abject and degraded present to wake up from their moral and spiritual slumber. Thus Dutt as a Bengali poet writing in English contributed a great deal to the Indian renaissance and reawakening.

In his poetry Soshee Chunder Dutt also attempts to recollect and re-embody the heroic figures from the past history of India. For example, his poem "Sivajee" records through a narrative the heroism of Shivaji who did not submit to the Mughul emperor Aurangzeb despite all physical tortures inflicted upon him. Though in bondage, Shivaji did not cower before Aurangzeb; rather Shivaji's sneer and hatred was manifest in his face:

He could not bear their servile scorn—
    The scorn of vassals low,
The passions of his stubborn heart
    Were gathering on his brow;
His bosom, plough'd with manly scars,
    The records of his fame,
Now heaved with all a warrior's wrath:
    He was not born to shame.[8]

Dutt delineates Shivaji's relentless efforts to oppose Aurangzeb and uphold the freedom of his land through fierce battles:

No, ne'er again he'll cross the hell
    To cringe on servile knee,
But oft, through battle's dusky smoke,
    His blood-red sword you'll see;
At merry feast he may not join,
    But through the war-clouds dun
O'er gasping chiefs and soldiers slain
    He'll lead the carnage on. (20)

The portrayal of patriotic figures from Indian history might have fanned the flame of patriotism in the heart of Soshee Chunder Dutt. His personal patriotism as revealed in his poetry will, however, be discussed in the next chapter.

Dutt exhibits his interest in the Hindu gods and goddesses in his poem *A Vision of Sumeru*. He describes the heavenly abodes of Shiva, Vishnu and Brahma in a detailed manner. The gods are represented as "quaffing the nectar sweet," served by Rati "the cupbearer of heaven".

In the poem Brahma tells the goddesses "Kamala, Kali and Uma wise" that "though men should cease to worship" them, they will still find "adorers" in heaven. The poet informs us that Ganesha is "the child of Uma's secret loves."

Though Dutt's references to the Hindu gods and goddesses are tangential to the main purpose of the poem, which is the assertion of faith in Christianity, it is to be noted that Dutt could not avoid the mention of those gods, as Hindu revivaliam, that is, a reawakening of interest in the Hindu religion, was very much in the air and was a part and parcel of the Renaissance movement in Bengal.

Among the contributors to the *Dutt Family Album*, Omesh Chunder Dutt has written several poems on the historical events of India. Even the titles of his poems indicate that their themes are taken from Indian history: "The Chief of Pokurna" "The Maid of Roopnagore", "The Death of Mohammad Ghori," "The Caves of Elephanta," "Jehangir's Lament," "To Lord Canning, during the Mutiny," "The Flight of Humaoon" and "The Flight of Rana Sanga."

"The Chief of Pokurna" is written under the inspiration of Todd's *Annals of Rajasthan*. It gives a spirited description of Pokurna's Lord:

> Not clad in steel, from head to heel
> In satin rich arrayed,
> With his trusty sword, Pokurna's Lord
> Is riding thro' the glade.[9]

In the poem entitled "The Flight of Rana Sanga," the poet describes how Rana Sanga faced the Moghul invaders though his Chiefs advised him to retreat:

> He gazed upon his chiefs and sighed, "This is a day of woe
> The Chohan flag did ne'er retreat before a conquering foe. (167)

In another poem "Caves of Elephanta," the poet describes how Time ravages the sculptures of the past embodying different deities of India, and notes with regret the natural sacrilege done to the statues of the deities:

> The snails on Brahma's forehead crawl
> The blind-worms dwell in Siva's eyes
> On Durga's cheek the rain drops fall—
> Or are they tears for days gone by? (66)

The greatest poet among the Bengalis writing in English during the nineteenth century to evoke and perpetuate in poetry the mythological locale, figures and zeitgeist of India's past is Toru Dutt. During the last years of her short life, after the period of her apprenticeship as a literary artist was over, she wrote her poems based on the Indian mythology. In those poems she not only recaptured the scenes of the past in vivid images but caught the very spirit of the legends from the *Ramayana*, the

Mahabharata and the *Puranas*. Very significantly, during the Bengal Renaissance, she recapitulated and embodied in her poems the fundamental moral values and the noble vision of life entertained by the Indians during the ancient times.

The striking quality of Toru Dutt's poems is that they not only present the situations and incidents of the legends graphically but also highlight the significant moral virtues that stood out in the popular outlook on life during those times. John B. Alphonso-Karkala has very pertinently remarked: "Toru gleaned tales and legends from the heroic past of India, approaching her task with reverence, and singing the tales as though they were "'so many intimate songs of her abiding faith' . . . Though they were inventions of the poets of the past, they had come down the ages as models of virtue meant to teach and delight—the collective conscience of the Indian people." (122) In the same vein, C. Paul Verghese comments: "It is true that Toru Dutt made an effort to reveal to the west the soul of India through the medium of poetry by narrating stories sung in divine poetry thousands of years ago." (29)

The first poem in *Ancient Ballads and Legends of Hindustan* is "Savitri." Based on a story from the *Mahabharata*, the poem narrates how Savitri, a woman of steadfast loyalty to her husband, wins back the life of Satyavan, her husband, from Yama, the King of Death, by establishing before the latter a unique example of sacrifice, devotion and loyalty to the man she has married. Being moved by Savitri's purity, integrity and loyalty of character, and unique boldness in pursuing Yama for recovering the life of her husband, Yama grants her prayer.

"Savitri" not only re-tells a myth, but also recreates a vision of life in which certain moral values were upheld. Savitri sets an example of unfailing steadfast loyalty of a wife to her husband in the face of all deadly adverse circumstances—this wifely virtue was regarded as the basic virtue of a married woman in ancient India. Toru Dutt recapitulates such moral virtues of ancient Indian life. Though Dutt makes an artistic presentation of the ancient myth, there is an implication that the virtues upheld in the myth are worthy of emulation even in modern times. The movement of the Bengal Renaissance was strengthened by the recapitulation of the virtues upheld in the ancient Indian life.

In Part I of the poem Dutt shows her awareness of the current social custom of keeping women in purdah and she contrasts the current constricting custom with the freedom and equality of status enjoyed by women in India in ancient days:

In those far-off primeval days
Fair India's daughters were not pent

In closed zenanas. On her ways
Savitri at her pleasure went
Whither she chose, hour by hour
With companions of her age,
She roamed the woods for fruit or flower,
Or loitered in some hermitage,
For to the Munis gray and old
Her presence was as sunshine glad,
They taught her wonders manifold
And gave her of the best they had.[10]

The stanza enshrines an impressive scene from ancient India which was conducive to the natural growth and development of womanhood with liberty, education and wisdom.

Reverence for pure womanhood and respect for the healthy growth of womanhood motivated Savitri's father to give Savitri all liberty and education:

Her father let her have her way
In all things, whether high or low;
He feared no harm; he knew no ill
Could touch a nature pure as snow. (110)

Dutt puts in a hint that people in ancient India believed that children were obtained through prayers to God:

Long childless, as a priceless boon
He had obtained this child at last
By prayers, made morning, night, and noon
With many a vigil, many a fast;
Would Shiva his own gift recall,
Or mar its perfect beauty ever? (110)

People of India in the classical past held firm views regarding their faith and beliefs.

Dutt pays a spontaneous tribute to the times when liberty and status were allowed to women at par with men:

And so she wandered where she pleased
In boyish freedom. Happy time! (110)

Thus nurtured into a beautiful and wise young woman, and given the right to choose her own bridegroom, Savitri chances upon Satyavan in a hermit's hut, and falls in love with him, though Satyavan no more enjoys royal glamour, as his father has been divested of his kingdom by his crooked opponents. Savitri's parents are given this information by her; and as they are wondering about the future, Narad Muni makes his appearance:

> As if the king's doubts to allay,
> Came Narad Muni to the place
> A few days after. Old and gray,
> All loved to see the gossip's face,
> Great Brahman's son,—adored of men,
> Long absent, doubly welcome he
> Unto the monarch, hoping then
> By his assistance, clear to see.
> No god in heaven, nor king on earth,
> But Narad knew his history,—
> The sun's, the moon's, the planets' birth
> Was not to him a mystery. (111)

The pristine faith of the ancient people of India permitted their imagination to visualize the appearance of gods and goddesses amongst the mortal men and women of the earth. Dutt recaptures this mythological faith in her ballads.

Savitri's character and actions have been exemplary right from the beginning. Though Narad Muni urges her to change her choice of the bridegroom, she does not change her mind as she thinks it would be a morally wrong action on her part. Her arguments bespeak her noble mind and character:

> And why should I? When I have given
> My heart away, though but in thought,
> Can I take back? Forbid it, Heaven!
> It were a deadly sin, I wot.
> And why should I? I know no crime
> In him or his. . . .
> . . . I cannot break
> A plighted faith, I cannot bear
> A wounded conscience. (112)

In these lines Savitri not only asserts her freedom of choice in the important issues of her life but also exhibits a constant consciousness of the profound dictates of her conscience. No doubt, such a character, as depicted by Dutt, must have appealed to the imagination of the Bengalis during the Renaissance.

The noble daughter, Savitri, has an equally noble father who gives his consent in the choice of such a groom in the following words:

> If wealth be gone, and kingdom lost,
> His merit still remains a star, . . .
> For riches, worldly power, or rank
> I care not,—I would have my son
> Pure, wise, and brave. (113)

Savitri's father upholds the merit of character in the groom as the only criterion of his choice, and not his rank or wealth. Dutt draws the attention of the Bengalis of the Renaissance period to the noble vision of life that was cherished by the ancient Indians.

Savitri settles the doubts and arguments on the choice of Satyavan as her groom, though Narad Muni foretells the death of Satyavan just a year after the marriage, by devoutly and staunchly following the dictates of her conscience in words that stir the heart and imagination of all:

> Once, and once only, have I given
> My heart and faith—'tis past recall; . . .
> Not the less solemn was my vow
> Because unheard, and oh! the sin
> Will not be less, if I should now
> Deny the feeling felt within. . . .
> The Right must be our guiding star;
> Duty our watchword, come what may. (114)

The integrity and faithfulness with which Savitri follows the dictates of her conscience and the unfailing courage and devotion with which she pursues the goal set before her makes her a remarkable woman worthy of emulation by all women in all the ages.

Though she has led the life of a princess before her marriage, Savitri does not flinch from the life of an ordinary woman residing in the hermit's hut. She rather illumines the husband's place:

> Savitri liked her new life much;
> Though in a lowly home she dwelt
> Her conduct as a wife was such
> As to illumine all the place;

She sickened not, nor sighed, nor pined;
But with simplicity and grace
Discharged each household duty kind.
Strong in all manual work,—and strong
To comfort, cherish, help, and pray,
The hours past peacefully along
And rippling bright, day followed day. (116)

Dutt's attempt to picturize an idealized sylvan life seems to be a reflection of the romantic idealism that characterized the Bengalis' philosophy of life during the nineteenth century.

After Satyavan passes away at the ordained moment, Savitri follows Yama as the latter takes away the soul of Satyavan. On the dark dreary way, Savitri, as she follows Yama, gives expression to certain wisdom which is based on the ancient Indian outlook upon life:

I know in such a world as this
No one can gain his heart's desire,
Or pass the years in perfect bliss;
Like gold we must be tried by fire;
And each shall suffer as he acts
And thinks,—his own sad burden bear.
Virtue should be the aim and end
Of every life, all else is vain,
Duty should be its dearest friend
If higher life it would attain. (124)

The vision of life, as presented by Dutt through the words of Savitri, is interpenetrated by moral aims: as a result the poem not only delights but also instructs. The poem is expressive of the philosophy of life upheld by the leaders of the Bengal Renaissance, as it handed down to them the rich cultural heritage of India.

The next poem, "Lakshman," is based on certain chapters in the *Ramayana*. In this poem Dutt portrays the loyalty of a young brother to his elder brother and sister-in-law; on the one hand, Lakshman tries to abide by Rama's dictates to protect Sita from all evils while Rama is away to catch the golden deer; on the other hand, Lakshman has to comfort his sister-in-law Sita who is agitated on hearing the death-cry in the imitated voice of Rama. Lakshman has to bear the harsh words of Sita because he does not want to violate his brother Rama's command:

For here beside thee, as a guard
    'Twas he commanded me to stay,
And dangers with my life to ward
    If they should come across thy way. (133)

When the integrity of his character is called in question, Lakshman cannot but yield to the pressure of Sita's emotional request to go away in search of Rama. However, he clarifies the situation by saying:

In going hence I disregard
    The plainest orders of my chief,
A deed for me,—a soldier,—hard
    And deeply painful, but thy grief
And language, wild and wrong, allow
    No other course. Mine be the crime,
And mine alone,—but oh, do thou
    Think better of me from this time. (135)

Under the given circumstances, the poet highlights the outstanding qualities of Lakshman's character—his sense of duty, his loyalty to his brother, his faithfulness to his sister-in-law, and self-sacrifice. These qualities of his character come to the fore when Lakshman finally leaves Sita after drawing a circle of safety around her:

Watch over Sita, whom alone
    I leave, and keep her safe from harm,
Till we return unto our own,
    I and my brother, arm in arm. (135)

Through this poem Dutt upholds certain virtues of family relationship that marked the picture of family bondage that held together Rama, Sita and Lakshman through years of suffering and adversity.

The next poem, "Jogadhya Uma," is a verse-tale about the appearance of Goddess Uma as a beautiful woman buying a bracelet from a bracelet pedlar who is asked to receive the price for the same from the priest of the temple where Uma is worshipped. The priest and the pedlar rush back to the spot where Uma appeared in the disguise of a beautiful woman but by then the beautiful woman has disappeared from there. On the priest's persistent supplication to the goddess, there appears only a sign:

Sudden from out the water sprung
A rounded arm, on which they saw
As high the lotus buds among
It rose, the bracelet white, with awe.
Then a wide ripple tost and swung
The blossoms on that liquid plain,
And lo! the arm so fair and young
Sank in the waters down again.
They bowed before the mystic Power.
And as they home returned in thought,
Each took from thence a lotus flower
In memory of the day and spot. (140)

The temple of Uma is thus hallowed by the divine appearance. Therefore, there developed the tradition of offering of shell-bracelets to the goddess by the pedlars of the same:

Years, centuries, have passed away,
And still before the temple shrine
Descendants of the pedlar pay
Shell-bracelets of the old design
As annual tribute. (141)

Though no moral design is discernible in the framework of this narrative, the poem succeeds in evoking the appropriate atmosphere for recreating the spirit and ethos of the age-old religious story.

"The Royal Ascetic and the Hind" is based on a story from the *Vishnu Purana*, Book II, Chapter XIII. This poem extols the power of love through the legend of Bharat, the great king of Saligram, who gives up all his wealth and worldly connections and becomes a hermit, but who cannot withdraw himself entirely from the overwhelming emotion of love that heaves through his heart as he nurses a hind in the forest. The poem concludes with a moral lesson:

God is Love, and not to be adored
By a devotion born of stoic pride,
Or with ascetic rites, or penance hard,
But with a love, in character akin
To his unselfish, all-including love. (144)

The poem is short but moving because of the details with which Dutt portrays the growth of love in the heart of the hermit-king for the poor delicate nursling hind.

"The Legend of Dhruva" is based on *Vishnu Purana*, Book I, Chapter XI. It narrates the story of Dhruva, the young son of King Uttanapado. Being denied the favour of his father as his step-mother wants to reserve all the royal favour for her own son, Uttama, Dhruva bears the insult silently and strives to reach a higher place, "a crown above my father's crown," and

> By prayer and penance Dhruva gained at last
> The highest heavens, and there he shines a star. (147)

The more striking part of the poem is that where Dhruva's mother advises Dhruva:

> That man is truly wise
> Who is content with what he has, and seeks
> Nothing beyond, but in whatever sphere,
> Lowly or great, God placed him, works in faith; . . .
> Be meek, devout, and friendly, full of love,
> Intent to do good to the human race
> And to all creatures sentient made of God;
> And oh, be humble, for on modest worth
> Descends prosperity, even as water flows
> Down to low grounds. (146-47)

The moral virtues, as enunciated by Dhruva's mother, are the virtues that were upheld and practised by Indians in the ancient times. Dutt has enshrined them in her poem for the people of the present times.

"Buttoo" is an interesting poem based on the story of Ekalavya in the *Mahabharata*. It narrates how Buttoo earns absolute proficiency in archery by learning the craft by himself with the ideal of the great master Dronacharya before him. Though Dronacharya, the teacher of the royal princess, declines to be the teacher of Buttoo, as he is just a hunter's son, Buttoo builds a clay statue of Dronacharya, whom he regards as his master. Dutt proclaims the great qualities of Buttoo's character that help him master the art of archery:

> By strained sense, by constant prayer,
> By steadfastness of heart and will,
> By courage to confront and dare,
> All obstacles he conquered still;
> A conscience clear,—a ready hand,
> Joined to a meek humility,

Success must everywhere command,
How could he fail who had all three! (151)

These moral virtues take him to a very high position in people's estimate; Dronacharya himself says after Buttoo shows his obedience to his guru by cutting off his thumb:

"For this,"—said Dronacharya,—"Fame
Shall sound thy praise from sea to sea,
And men shall ever link thy name
With Self-help, Truth, and Modesty." (153)

Inspired by the impulse to re-awaken Indians' pride in their own rich cultural heritage, Dutt has re-created in her poetry these noble and exemplary characters who have attained greatness and grandeur through the practice of virtues and nobility in life.

"Sindhu" is based on the episode of Shravankumar in the *Ramayana*. King Dasarath unwittingly killed Sindhu, the young son of an old hermit couple, while Sindhu was filling up the pitcher with water behind a screen of trees for his parents who would break fast that evening.

The episode is narrated with interesting details. The character of Sindhu stands out: first, he is the outstanding example of a son devoted to the service of his blind parents:

Attentive, duteous, loving, kind,
Thoughtful, sedate, and calm,
He waited on his parents blind,
Whose days were like psalm.

He roamed the woods for luscious fruits,
He brought them water pure,
He cooked their simple mess of roots,
Content to live obscure. (154)

Secondly, Sindhu shows exemplary restraint when he refrains from bestowing any curse on King Dasarath:

No curses, no!—I bear no grudge,
Not thou my blood has spilt,
Lo! here before the unseen Judge,
Thee I absolve from guilt. (158)

Here, again, in this moving verse-tale, Dutt shows the nobility of character cherished and treasured in the great epics of India.

In "Prahlad" Dutt narrates how Prahlad persists in his devotion to God despite the tyrannical father's order for his execution. When asked by the tyrant father what is true knowledge, Prahlad answers,

> That is true knowledge which can make
> Us mortals saintlike, holy, pure,
> The strange thirst of the spirit slake
> And strengthen suffering to endure. (166)

Thereafter, Prahlad is threatened and subjected to several attempts of murder but he is saved by God because of his steadfast devotion:

> There is one God—One Only—mark!
> To Him is all our service due.
>
> Hath He a shape, or hath He none?
> I know not this, nor care to know,
> Dwelling in light, to which the sun
> Is darkness, He sees all below,
> Himself unseen! In Him I trust,
> He can protect me if He will. (169)

Ultimately, the Evil as embodied in the tyrant Heerun Kasyapu the King is destroyed by the messenger of God, and Prahlad is installed as the King to begin the reign of the good. The ultimate victory of the good over the evil is an important teaching enshrined in the age-old tales of India. Through all these verse-tales of *Ancient Ballads and Legends of Hindustan*, Dutt proves herself to be the first major Indian English poet to deal with the themes from Indian mythology extensively for preservation of cardinal human values cherished in India in ancient times.

The other great poet who explored extensively in Indian mythology and spiritual heritage is Sri Aurobindo. His most important works, however, appeared in the twentieth century. Still the poems that he wrote in the nineteenth century deal at length with several episodes from the Indian mythology. They also justifiably testify to C. Paul Verghese's remark on his poetic output as a whole: "the bulk of his poetic output has about it an aroma of the spirituality of India and is as much an expression of a personal vision as that of the spiritual personality of India." (61)

As Aurobindo touched the shore of India on his return from England in 1893, he underwent a profound spiritual experience which he himself described: "Since I set foot on the Indian soil on the Apollo Bunder in Bombay, I began to have spiritual experiences, but these were not divorced from this world but had an inner and infinite bearing on it, such as a feeling of Infinite pervading material Space and the Immanent inhabiting material objects and bodies."[11]

In one of his early poems, "Perfect Thy Motion," Sri Aurobindo gives a hint of the spiritual stirrings within his inner being:

> Perfect thy motion ever within me,
> Master of mind.
> Grey of the brain, flash of the lightning,
> Brilliant and blind,
> These thou linkest, the world to mould,
> Writing the thought in a scroll of gold
> Violet-lined.[12]

Sri Aurobindo's spiritual perception of the presence of the Supreme Lord in every object of the universe and within his own soul refers us back to the spiritual heritage of India as embodied in the *Upanishads*.

Sri Aurobindo's early interest in the Indian mythology accounts for the later development of his interest in Indian spirituality. One of his early poems, "To a Hero-Worshipper," clearly indicates his interest in the past of India:

> I by the Indian waters vast
> Did glimpse the magic of the past
> And on the oaten-pipe I play
> Warped echoes of an earlier day. (8)

Indian mythology and religious legends appealed to Sri Aurobindo's imagination. Even in the early years of his youth he exhibits in his poetry a close familiarity with the legendary and mythological past of India. The early poem "Envoi" indicates the depth of his faith in the religious and mythological vision of India:

> Me from her lotus heaven Saraswati
> Has called to regions of eternal snow
> And Ganges pacing to the southern sea,
> Ganges upon whose shores the flowers of Eden blow. (28)

Sri Aurobindo's insight into the mysterious world of the Indian mythology is accompanied by his imaginative grasp of each minute detail of that world which he elaborately evokes in his poetry. "Urvasie" is a long poem of about 1500 lines, divided in four cantos, about the ecstasy and agony of Pururavus's profound love of Urvasie who dropped from the heaven and then vanished back into it to put Pururavus on a constant quest of his lost love. Sri Aurobindo explores the myth with extraordinary sensitivity in line after line of haunting beauty.

Manoj Das indicates the source of the story: "Among the poems written during the Baroda period is *Urvasie* inspired by Kalidasa's recreation of the eternal nymph of the *Rig Veda*, the story of the 'goddess won to mortal arms.'" (23) M.K. Naik is more specific on this point: "'Urvasie' is a retelling of the ancient Indian legend of King Pururavus and his love for the celestial damsel, Urvasie—a legend immortalized by Kalidasa in his play, Vikramorvasie." (48)

King Pururavus hints about his mystical perception of the woman who will visit him and make his dream of love come true:

> Wast thou not a part
> Of soft auspicious evenings I have loved?
> Have I not seen thy beauty on the clouds?
> In moonlight and in starlight and in fire?
> Some flower whose brightness was a trouble? a face
> Whose memory like a picture lived with me?
> A thought I had, but lost? O was thy voice
> A vernal repetition in some grove,
> Telling of lilies clustered o'er with bees
> And quiet waters open to the moon? (191)

The poem is replete with such descriptions of emotional quests where the spirit rises above the perception of the mere physical to the higher level of a realization of the abstract. Though written in blank verse, the poem reaches a lyrical height where the whole span of Time and Space is constantly traversed, and every syllable sounds magical:

> And I perceive our union magically
> Inevitable as a perfect verse
> Of Veda. (191)

Canto I ends with the description of Pururavus returning from heavenly tour to his own home-town upon the earth. On the way, after the disappearance of the heavenly figures like "Menaca, Misracayshie, Mullica/Rumbha, Nelabha, Shela, Nolinie/Lolita, Lavonya and Tilottama" (190):

He [Pururavus], the sole living,
Over the deep-plunging precipices
Passed bright and small in a wide dazzling world
Illimitable, where eye flags and ear
Listening feels inhuman loneliness.
He tended towards Gangotri's solemn peaks
And savage glaciers and the caverns pure
Whence Ganges leaps, our mother, virgin-cold. (196)

Aurobindo's mythopoeic imagination recreates the scenes and situations of the legend with a clarity and vividness that makes the whole myth come alive before the eyes of his readers.

Sri Aurobindo's art of description is excellent. With his delicate use of choice words, and absolute mastery over rhythm and metrical pattern, he presents image after image which may be mistaken for either a painting or a sculpture or a piece of life transformed into a piece of art. Urvasie, being banished by Bharuth, takes leave of the beautiful paradise:

Under
Green well-known boughs laden with nameless fruit
And over blissful swards and perfect flowers
And through the wandering alleys she arrived
To heavenly Ganges where it streams o'er stones;
There from the banks of summer downward stopped,
One little golden hand gathering her dress
Above her naked knees, and, lovely, passed
Through the divine pellucid river on
To Swarga's portals, pausing on the slope
Which goes toward the world. (200-1)

Sri Aurobindo's poetic art vivifies the whole scene—an art that is reminiscent of the mythological art and imagination of the ancient poets of India.

The love between King Pururavus of the earth and Urvasie of the heaven is presented through the enchanting warp and woof of Sri Aurobindo's poetry that transforms the dream and vision of the myth into a perceptible reality:

His [Pururavus's] words that first
Dreamed like a languid wave, sudden were foam;
And he beheld her standing and his look
Grew strong; he yearned towards her like a wave,

And she received him in her eyes as earth
Receives the rain. (205)

Canto II ends with the union between Pururavus and Urvasie, enacted through words that harmoniously symbolize the combination of the earthy and the celestial, the sensual and the spiritual.

The first part of Canto III describes through vivid poetic details the seven years of Urvasie's stay in Pururavus's palace. The ancient poets of India always visualized constant exchanges between the earth and the paradise, and their spacious imagination frequently shifted from the particular to the universal and from the terrestrial to the cosmic. Their capacity to shift from the microcosm to the macrocosm is reflected in Sri Aurobindo's presentation of the Urvasie legend. He does not confine his vision to Pururavus and the people of Ila while describing the sojourn of Urvasie in Pururavus's palace, but in a glorious sweep he states that the whole earth enjoyed the stay of Urvasie:

Seven years the earth rejoiced in Urvasie. (210)

Urvasie was taken back to the heaven while Pururavus was asleep. His discovery of this desertion is presented in a cluster of monosyllables that ring with indescribable pathos:

But the grey dawn came in
And raised his lashes. He stretched out his arms
To find her. Then he knew he was alone. (214)

Canto III ends with the crowning of Urvasie's son:

Then was brought forth the bud of Urvasie,
With Vedic verse intoned and Ganges pure
Was crowned a king, and empire on his curls
Established. (218)

Then Pururavus takes leave of Ila's town, and disappears "from light/Into forest."

In Canto IV, Pururavus wanders through the forest where he lived with Urvasie just after she dropped down from the heaven. Pururavus's reminiscence is evocative and tinged with sorrow:

O once she was the luminous soul of these,
And in her body lived the summer and spring

And seed and blossoming, ripening and fall,
Hiding of Beauty in the wood and glen,
And flashing out into the sunlit fields
All flowers and laughter. (220)

This canto describes the endless quest accompanied by the meditation for the recovery of the lost Urvasie. Pururavus is presented as a monk in meditation:

Long he, in meditation deep immersed,
Strove to dissolve his soul among the hills
Into the thought of Urvasie. The snow
Stole down from heaven and touched his cheek and hair,
The storm-blast from the peaks leaped down and smote
But woke him not. (221)

Of course, he is charged by Luxmie for the neglect of his duty to his kingdom.

However, some other goddesses express extreme joy in the things of the earth:

O one day I shall turn from the great verse
And marble aspiration to sing sweetly
Of lovers and the pomps of wealth and wine
And warm delights and warm desires and earth. (225)

In the days of the Bengal Renaissance it was very significant that Sri Aurobindo chose a theme in the elaboration of which he could show the gods' and goddesses' passion for the earth. The Renaissance thinkers not only thought of the earth as the best place for living but also imagined that the earth could bring down the paradise upon itself. The poem, *Urvasie*, indicates Sri Aurobindo's sharing in this Renaissance idealization of the human life.

As Pururavus drank the "wonderful water of the lake" within "the hollow of her [Aryans' mother-goddess'] hand," he

. . . understood infinity, and saw
Time like a snake coiling among the stars;
And earth he saw, and mortal nights and days
Grew to him moments, and his limbs became
Undying and his thoughts as marble endured. (225)

That man has infinite power is a Renaissance idea: and Sri Aurobindo has incorporated that idea in his exposition of the Pururavus legend. And that man can make himself immortal by the pursuit of a goal which has infinite possibilities is suggested when Aryans' mother-goddess addresses Pururavus as "O strong immortal." (225)

Though Pururavus is granted the pursuit of his joy in Urvasië, the Goddess foretells the long lineage of the Aryan kings descending from him:

> Empire shall in thy line and forceful brain
> Persist, the boundless impulse towards rule
> Of grandiose souls perpetually recur,
> And minds immense and personalities
> With battle and with passion and with storm
> Shall burn through Aryan history, the speech
> Of ages. (226)

Thus Sri Aurobindo incorporates history in the myth and turns the mythological content into a symbolic parable which is further authenticated by the introduction of history. Hence, Sri Aurobindo's poem, "Urvasie," may be looked upon as an epitome of the third characteristic of the Bengal Renaissance, as stated in the third chapter, namely, the rediscovery of the glorious past of India.

That the poem, "Urvasie," is written with a direct spontaneous participation in the meaningful legend is evident in the lucid artistic lyricism that accompanies Sri Aurobindo's description and exposition at every stage. When the final union between Pururavus and Urvasie is accomplished, the poet depicts the union with perfect artistic mastery:

> There by a sounding river downward thrown
> From under low green-curtaining boughs was she.
> Mute she arose and with wide quiet eyes
> Came towards him. In their immortal looks
> Was a deep feeling too august for joy,
> The sense that all eternity must follow
> One perfect moment. (227)

Sri Aurobindo is the finest product of the Bengal Renaissance movement to have written English poetry which has India and her values and philosophy as embodied in her epics, the *Puranas* and the scriptures, as the background as well as the central inspiration.

The next poem, "Love and Death," is a long poem of about 1100 lines without, however, any division into cantos. Sri Aurobindo himself indicates the source and theme of the poem in a letter: "The story of Ruru and Pramadvura—I have substituted a name [Priyumvada] more manageable to the English tongue—her death in the forest by the snake and restoration at the price of half her husband's life is told in the *Mahabharata*. It is a companion legend to the story of Savitri." (258)

In contrast to the description of love between Urvasie and Pururavus, where a heavenly figure is involved, the description of love between Ruru and Priyumvada is less inspiring and moving. The love in this poem is described in more sensuous and earthy images. At long intervals, however, Sri Aurobindo's lyricism bursts forth. Moreover, Sri Aurobindo, the father-figure of the Bengal Renaissance, perceived the infinite and the divine as a part of the finite and the mundane to such a profound extent that his description is always, in some way or the other, shot through by the flashes of the divine: a quality which may be attributed to the Renaissance tendency towards the idealization and glorification of life. For example, this quality is discernible when Sri Aurobindo describes Ruru's personality as a lover:

And Ruru felt
The sweetness of the early earth as sap
All through him, and short life an aeon made
By boundless possibility, and love,
Sweetest of all unfathomable love,
A glory untired. (230)

On the other hand, this poem abounds in the use of sensuous images for the presentation of love between Ruru and Priyumvada:

She all fresh and new
Rose to him, and he plunged into her charm.
For neither to her honey and poignancy
Artlessly interchanged, nor any limit
To the sweet physical delight of her
He found. (232)

But as pointed out earlier, Sri Aurobindo could not be content with the description of the sensuous and the fleshly. He, being a Renaissance man, glorified the sensual pleasure by using allusions to the heaven. He describes the physical charms of Priyumvada,

. . . the ravishing realm of her white limbs,

An empire for the glory of a God. (232)

The tussle between life and death, and after the struggle, the victory of life over death, seem to be a theme of profound interest to the Bengali poets writing in English during the nineteenth century. The story of Savitri winning over the life of Satyavan from Yama was dealt with at great length by Toru Dutt. In "Love and Death," Sri Aurobindo dwells on the paradoxical juxtaposition of life and death, and the undying wish of love for eternity in the face of dreadful death. The poet puts in the mouth of Ruru words of distinctive Renaissance craving for infinitude and eternity in the enjoyment of love and beauty:

"O father Sun,"
He [Ruru] cried, "how good it is to live, to love!
Surely our joy shall never end, nor we
Grow old, but like bright rivers or pure winds
Sweetly continue, or revive with flowers,
Or live at least as long as senseless trees. (233)

However, the pathos of a life shortened by sudden death is very movingly evoked through the words of dying Priyumvada:

I was so glad of love and kisses
And thought that centuries would not exhaust
The deep embrace. And I have had so little
Of joy and the wild day and throbbing night,
Laughter, and tenderness, and strife and tears. (235)

Sri Aurobindo maintains the continuity of the narrative, but interpolates Renaissance ideas in the fabric of the narrative. Thus the poem presents the ideas of the Bengal Renaissance in an artistic manner.

There is an imaginary conversation between the grief-stricken Ruru and Kama, the god of love. Sri Aurobindo highlights the persistent effort and continuous penitence of Ruru to reach and win back Priyumvada from the kingdom of Death. Sri Aurobindo mixes the myth with the history and geography of India. He maps out the wandering quest of Ruru:

But from Shatudru and Bipasha, streams
Once holy, and loved Iravathi and swift
Clear Chandrabhaga and Bitosta's toil
For man, went Ruru to bright sumptuous lands

By Aryan fathers not yet paced. (246)

Ruru goes through the horrible scenes in the Hell in his endless search for his beloved. He cannot pause in his search as

terrible strong love
Was like a fiery finger in his breast
Pointing him on. (248)

Ruru passes through the labyrinthine torture chambers of the *Patala*, that is, the underworld, and suffer the gruesome hideous sights:

Twelve times he crossed
Boithorini, the river dolorous,
Twelve times resisted Hell
. . . —punishments
Whose sight pollutes, unheard-of tortures, pangs
Monstrous, intolerable mute agonies,
Twisted unmoving attitudes of pain. (256)

After wading through the phantasmagoric nightmares of the horrid underworld, Ruru ultimately wins Priyumvada, and is rewarded with the happy sweet life:

Thrilling he felt beneath his bosom her;
Oh, warm and breathing were those rescued limbs
Against the greenness, vivid, palpable, white,
With great black hair and real and her cheek's
Old softness and her mouth a dewy rose. (257)

"Love and Death" is a vindication of the power of love, and of the endless pleasures of the earthly life. By recapturing these lessons from the mythical legend of Ruru and Pramadvura, Sri Aurobindo has used the vehicle of poetry for the perpetuation of the Renaissance respect for love and life.

The next poem "The Rishi" is in the form of a dialogue between King Manu and the Rishi about the goal of man's knowledge. The poem has a perfect metrical form, but the aridity of the dialectics prevents it from being an interesting poetic composition. However, the old Indian idea of man's consciousness and inner being as enveloped by a veil of delusion is indicated by the last answer given by the Rishi to the question of King Manu:

For thou art He, O King. Only the night
Is on thy soul
By thy own will. Remove it and recover
The serene whole
Thou art indeed, then raise up man the lover
To God the goal. (311-12)

India's spiritual ideas about God in man, as propounded in the *Vedas* and *Upanishads*, are dealt with in this poem.

Sri Aurobindo presents the theme of Chitrangada in the next poem entitled "Chitrangada," but as the poem is just a fragment, it does not develop into a full poem. It contains a dialogue between Chitrangada and Urjoon reminiscing about their first encounter.

The next poem "Ulopie" is also a fragment. It continues the Urjoon and Chitrangada story from the earlier poem. The poem has no more significance than a plain narrative in which Chitrangada's impending desertion by Urjoon is delineated through a dialogue between the two. Chitrangada's concluding remarks to the horses of Urjoon's war-chariot is a sad evocative conclusion of the poem:

O horses yoked to fate. How often yet
Will you deceive us shaking wide your manes
And trampling over some women's hearts with hooves
Thunderous towards battle? (332)

The last fragment in blank verse written by Sri Aurobindo before the close of the nineteenth century is "The Tale of Nala" which is based on an episode from the *Mahabharata*. The poem begins and ends in beautiful description, but cannot develop the theme as the poem is left incomplete by the poet. Nala imprisons an Apsara in the form of a swan, and will not let her go back to the heaven. The Apsara appreciates the beauty and courage of King Nala:

Because thou art bright and beautiful and bold,
So have I come to thee and thou hast seized
Whom if thou hadst set free, thy joy were lost,
So in thy mind from some celestial space
A name and face have come, yet are on earth,
Which if thou hadst not held with yearning's stays,
Thy mortal life would have been given in vain,
Forced by thy musing in the sapphire noon
Out of the mountains's breast to thee I flew. (338)

Sri Aurobindo's poetry written during the nineteenth century is remarkable on account of its masterly handling of the themes from the Indian mythology. The worth of his poetry written during this period is heightened by his embodiment of the philosophy of life, love and death, cherished by the poets and seers of ancient India.

Swami Vivekananda is the last poet of the nineteenth century to have given expression to the spiritual quest of ancient India. Himself a Yogi, Vivekananda was spiritually endowed to understand and appreciate the spiritual past of India. He, however, wrote only a few lyrics—but they give an authentic embodiment to his profound spiritual perception and realization. His quest in poetry may be treated as a legacy of the spiritual past of India. It should be borne in mind that he contributed to the spiritual regeneration of Bengal during the nineteenth century.

His first poem "Kali the Mother" portrays through vivid images the essential spirit of Kali the goddess who came as the destroyer of the evil. The poet enthusiastically celebrates the goddess of destruction:

Dancing mad with joy,
    Come, Mother, come!
For terror is Thy name,
    Death is in Thy breath.

And every shaking step
    Destroys a world for e'er.
Thou "Time," the All-Destroyer!
    Come, O Mother, come![13]

In "To the Awakened India," Vivekananda remembers the gods and goddesses of India and the philosophy of the Truth, the One and the Infinite Love:

And all above,
    Himala's daughter Uma, gentle, pure,
    The Mother that resides in all as Power
    And Life, who works all works and
    Makes of One the world, whose mercy
    Opens the gate to Truth and shows
    The One in All, give thee untiring
    Strength, which is Infinite Love. (388)

Though the poetic richness of Sri Aurobindo's verse is not there in the lines quoted above, they state emphatically and forcefully

Vivekananda's perception of the eternal truth of India as envisaged in the ancient scriptures.

Vivekananda's insistence on the soul as opposed to the flesh is a legacy from India's hoary past. In the poem, "Requiescat in Pace," Vivekananda addresses the soul, and wishes the soul godspeed as it is not bound by the limits of time and space:

> Speed forth, O Soul! upon thy star-strewn path;
> Speed, blissful one! where thought is ever free,
> Where time and space no longer mist the view,
> Eternal peace and blessings be with thee! (389)

"The Song of the Sannyasin" is a well-wrought poem where the poet vindicates the supremacy of the Self, that is, the Upanishadic precept of "Know Thyself" as the ultimate truth and goal of life. The last stanza contains the essence of the age-old philosophy of India:

> Thus, day by day, till Karma's powers spent
> Release the soul for ever. No more is birth,
> Nor I, nor thou, nor God, nor man. The "I"
> Has all become, the All is "I" and Bliss.
> Know thou art That, Sannyasin bold! Say—
> "Om Tat Sat, Om!" (395)

Vivekananda has been able to put into a poetic form the precepts of the Vedas and Upanishads in which he had firm faith. Thus his poetry becomes a perfect embodiment of the philosophy of ancient India.

In this chapter I have tried to show that all the leading Bengali poets writing in English during the nineteenth century have resuscitated the glory of the past of India in their poetry in order to revive the memory of the Bengalis during the Renaissance period as regards their own rich cultural heritage. This inevitably added a stimulus to the development and propagation of the Renaissance movement in Bengal.

NOTES

1. H.L.V. Derozio, *Poems* (Calcutta, 1980), p. 1.
2. Pallav Sengupta, *Kavi Derozio* (Calcutta, 1982), p. 31.
3. V.K. Gokak, *The Golden Treasury of Indo-Anglian Poetry* (New Delhi, 1978), p. 9.

4. H.M. Williams, *Indo-Anglian Literature* (Madras, 1976), p. 17.
5. C. Paul Verghese, *Problems of the Indian Creative Writer in English* (Bombay, 1971), p. 19.
6. *Madhusudan Rachanavali* (Calcutta, 1982), p. 487.
7. John B. Alphonso-Karkala, *Indo-English Literature in the Nineteenth Century* (Mysore, 1970), p. 49.
8. V.K. Gokak, p. 18.
9. *Dutt Family Album* (London, 1870), p. 10.
10. Toru Dutt, *Ancient Ballads and Legends of Hindustan*, ed. A.N. Dwivedi (Bareilly, 1976), p. 109.
11. Qtd. Manoj Das, *Sri Aurobindo* (New Delhi, 1982), p. 16.
12. Sri Aurobindo, *Collected poems* (Pondicherry, 1972), p. 7.
13. *The Complete Works of Swami Vivekananda* (Calcutta, 1978), Vol. IV, p. 348.

Nationalism and Patriotism

The fourth characteristic that marks the Bengal Renaissance is the intense nationalism and patriotism of all the Bengalis inspired by the Renaissance movement. The discovery of the glorious past of India together with a new awareness of the same led to the resurgence of nationalism and patriotism among all the Bengalis during this period. This finds an eloquent expression in the nineteenth-century English poetry of Bengal.

Derozio is the first poet of the nineteenth century to give utterance to intense nationalism and patriotism. Though a European by birth, Derozio, according to Srinivasa Iyengar, was "wholly Indian in spirit and aspired to be India's national bard."[1]

Derozio is not only the first patriot of the Bengal Renaissance period but the first champion of reason and progressive ideas in his national and patriotic outlook. R.K. Dasgupta aptly remarks: "Henry Louis Vivian Derozio is modern India's first patriot to give expression to that patriotism in verse, the first to sing of Freedom 'that lights the altar of the soul with everlasting flame,' the first to contemplate an intellectual renaissance for an ancient civilization through 'new perceptions,' the first to exalt reason as an instrument of progress."[2] Derozio saw a new vision of new India. He not only loved the country but also imagined a luminous future for her.

Derozio's poem, "The Harp of India," powerfully embodies his passionate commitment to India. He perceives the decay of India's tradition deeply, and describes graphically the state of decadence when he evokes the image of the harp of India unstrung "on yon withered bough." (1) He aspires to belong to the great tradition of Indian poets of the past when he puts in his sincere supplication:

> Harp of my country, let me strike the strain! (1)

Commenting on the line, John B. Alphonso-Karkala remarks: "Unlike his Eurasian community, which clung more to Europe and the ruling class than to India and her masses, Henry boldly asserts his Indianness in his last dramatic line."[3]

"To India—My Native Land" is a more direct expression of Derozio's patriotic fervour. His sorrow at the spectacle of decay in the country finds a poignant expression when he laments,

> Where is that glory, where that reverence now? (2)

The poet's wrath and grief at the servile bondage of India is imaged forth when he describes the ignominous condition of India under the British rule:

> Thy eagle pinion is chained down at last,
> And grovelling in the lowly dust art thou:
> Thy mistrel hath no wreath to weave for thee
> Save the sad story of thy misery! (2)

The poet is determined to revive from the depth of oblivion the classic past of India. The poet's retrospective glimpse of his country is expressive of his zealous patriotism:

> Well—let me dive into the depths of time,
> And bring from out the ages that have rolled
> A few small fragments of those wrecks sublime,
> Which human eye may never more behold. (2)

R.K. Dasgupta's comment on the last two lines of the poem is relevant: "What gives this sonnet 'To India—My Native Land' its significance in the history of Indian patriotism is that it is more than a paean of our ancient glory: it is also a vow of service to the country:

> And let the guerdon of my labour be
> My fallen country! one kind wish from thee! (vi)

Derozio's vision of a new India, free from superstition and ignorance, blooming and growing with fresh energy and unclouded intellectual powers is recorded in his "Sonnet to the Pupils of the Hindu College." A teacher of the Hindu College, Derozio found that the vision of a new India was being realized through the efforts of his young students who represented the new generation of India. Comparing his students, to whom he has imparted the new ideas of Europe and America, to young flowers whose petals are opening out, he hopes that with their "intellectual energies and powers," they would be able to shake themselves out of the octopus nexus of the superstitions and useless customs that crippled the life of the Bengalis during the last three centuries.

That the young students of the Hindu College are gathering strength and hope under the stimulus of new learning and knowledge imparted to them by Derozio and other enlightened teachers of the College is poetically indicated when Derozio compares them to young birds:

> That stretch (like young birds in soft summer hours)
> Their wings, to try their strength. (43)

Derozio imaginatively portrays the influence of new knowledge from abroad upon the young minds of the students and their steadfast devotion to the cause of Truth:

> O, how the winds
> Of circumstances, and freshening April showers
> Of early knowledge, and unnumbered kinds
> Of new perceptions shed their influence;
> And how you worship truth's omnipotence (43)

These students are looked upon as a symbol of hope for new India. Thus the vision of the future India brings joy to the heart of Derozio, and he sings in joy:

> What joyance rains upon me, when I see
> Fame in the mirror of futurity. (43)

Derozio thinks of his life to be a successful one as he has been able to teach these new Hindus to open out their minds to the unprejudiced and scientific ideas of the West, and then, lay the foundation of a new India:

> Ah then I feel I have not lived in vain! (43)

R.K. Dasgupta is very much right when he remarks: "In 'To India—My Native Land' and 'Sonnet to the Pupils of the Hindu College' we have for the first time in Indian writing a hymn to ancient India and a dream of her renaissance." (vi) M.K. Naik pays rich tribute to Derozio as a patriot-poet: "A noteworthy feature of Derozio's poetry is its burning nationalistic zeal. . . . Poems like 'To India—My Native Land,' 'The Harp of India,' and 'To the Pupils of the Hindu College' have an unmistakable authenticity of patriotic utterance which stamps Derozio as an

Indian English poet who is truly a son of the soil."[4]

Kasiprasad Ghose exhibits his love of the native land, India or more precisely Bengal, in his poem, "The Shair's Farewell Song." The poet offers a moving description of the native land to which the shair has to bid farewell:

Farewell my lovely native land!
　　Where roses bloom in many a vale;
Where green-clad hills majestic stand,
　　Where flowerets woo the scented gale,
Where Surya from his throne above
　　With brightest colours paints the day;
Where ripplets rise to clasp their love,
The eluding beams that o'er them play.[5]

Ghose's description displays his fascination with the natural beauty of his country and also his awareness of the greatness of his country:

Land of the Gods and lofty name;
　　Land of the fair and beauty's spell;
Land of the bards of mighty fame;
　　My native land! fore'er farewell. (9)

This poem embodies the poet's nationalism and patriotism.

Gooroo Churn Dutt exhibits his deeply-felt love of his country when he pays tribute to his motherland. His poem, "Introductory Lines," is short but no less significant on account of its sense of patriotism:

And hail thee, India, from thy days of yore,
Then welcome to my breast, forever dear,
While on thy sad remains I drop a tear.
And tho' I'm born in this unlucky age,
Without the fire of any ancient sage,
Accept the tribute of a heart sincere. (9)

The poet's sadness at the present condition of his motherland makes him more sympathetic to the cause of his country.

Michael Madhusudan Dutt's nationalism and patriotism find expression in the narrative poem, "King Porus," where he presents an admirable portrait of King Porus who was an upright and unfailing lover of freedom and never bowed down to a foreign invader. Dutt pays rich tribute to the soldiers in King Porus's army who sacrificed their lives for the defence of the freedom and sovereignty of their motherland:

Fell India's hardy sons,—
Proud mountain oaks by thunders riven,—
That for their country's freedom bled—
And made on gore their glorious bed! (14)

While recounting the heroic story of King Porus's fight against Alexander's army, the poet chooses words that highlight the greatness of India's brave warrior:

He [Porus] reck'd not of the phalanx
That 'round him closed—but nobly fought,
And like the angry winds that blow
And lofty mountain pines lay low,
Amidst them dreadful havoc wrought,
And thinn'd his crown and country's foe! (15)

Alexander was so impressed by the heroism of King Porus that he asked his soldiers not to hit blows on him:

'Desist desist!'—he cried—
'Such noble blood should not be shed!' (15)

When King Porus is brought before Alexander the Emperor,

He stooped not—bent not there his knee,—
But stood, as stands an oak,
In Himalayan majesty. (16)

At the end of the narrative, Dutt laments the passing away of such heroes from the country. With sorrow and anger, the poet asks:

But where, oh! where is Porus now?
And where the noble hearts that bled
For freedom—with the heroic glow
In patriot bosoms nourished—
—Hearts, eagle-like that recked not death,
But shrank before foul Thraldom's breath? (16-17)

Dutt's nationalism and patriotism find an ardent expression in the afterthought added to the poem:

> And where are thou—Fair Freedom!—thou
> Once goddess of Ind's sunny clime!
> When glory's halo round her brow
> Shone radiant, and the rose sublime,
> Like her own towering Himalye,
> To kiss the blue clouds thron'd on high! (17)

Dutt's profound love of India and her freedom is reflected in his portrayal of King Porus's battle against the foreign invader.

Shoshee Chunder Dutt's sonnet "India" expresses the poet's love of the country, his desire for the freedom of the country, and his dream about the future development of the country:

> I dreamt a dream of strange and wild delight,
> Freedom's pure shrine once more illumed dim seem,
> The clouds had pass'd beneath the morning light;
> On beauty's cheek I mark'd the tear-drops dry,
> And sighs and groans for ever fled the land;
> Science again aspired to the sky,
> And patriot valour watch'd the smiling strand:
> A dream! a dream! Why should a dream it be?
> Land of my fathers! Canst thou ne'er be free? (20-21)

It is interesting to note that these poets of the Bengal Renaissance movement not only dreamed about the future but looked forward to the scientific development of their motherland.

Hur Chuder Dutt, a contributor to the *Dutt Family Album*, has written a sonnet entitled "India," where he expresses nationalistic feelings and displays sincere patriotism. The poem begins with an avowal of the poet's love of the country:

> O yes! I love thee with a boundless love,
> Land of my birth. (26)

The flame of discontent at the degradation of his motherland burns in the poet's heart:

> . . . and while I lisp thy name,
> Burns in my soul 'an Aetna of pure flame'

Which none can quench nor naught on earth remove. (26)

The poet recapitulates the "days of glory" and "soldiers live, for thee dear land who fell." The moment the poet thinks on the bondage of India, he wakes "to mourn," and "in poor lays thy widowed fate deplore." Still the poet's patriotism inspires him to envisage a brighter future for his motherland:

. . . though these decay,
I see broad streaks of a still brighter day. (26)

The more well-known poet, Toru Dutt, died at an early age of twenty-one. During the period of her short life she travelled to several countries of Europe. But though brought up as a Christian, and educated mainly in European arts and culture, she shows in her poetry a genuine love of her motherland. In her *Ancient Ballads and Legends of Hindustan*, Dutt evinces the inner core of her nationalism and patriotism through her choice of ancient legends and myths of India for poetic treatment.

In her shorter lyrical poem, "Our Casuarina Tree," Dutt expresses directly her infatuation with her own motherland. When she is abroad, she remembers with nostalgia the casuarina tree in the compound of her house in Calcutta. The following lines from the poem are not only evocative but expressive of her deep love of her native country:

O Tree, as in my happy prime,
I saw thee, in my own loved native clime.[6]

Her deep-seated love of her "Own loved naive clime" finds mature expression in her sensitive exposition of Indian myths in the longer poems of *Ancient Ballads and Legends of Hindustan*.

Manmohan Ghose spent his early childhood and youth in England. Though he was far away from his motherland, and brought up in English environment, his mind yearned for India, the country where he was born. Though most of his poems are about nature and love, there lie embedded in them, here and there, references to India that speak volumes of his love of the country.

In a love poem, "Myvanwy," Ghose's love of his country may be traced very distinctly. He tells his beloved:

Yes, o'er that ocean far, far in the distance,
Is my own country, and other soil bore me

Than thy dear birthplace, other sun than England's
Nourished my spirit.[7]

The poet goes on describing his country to his English beloved: the description betrays the poet's keen attachment to the country of his origin:

There, stretching lonely, do the giant mountains
Rise with their ages of snows to heaven,
Snows, the heart shudders, so far away seem they,
Fearfully lovely. (41)

The poem is not only about the poet's love of the English maiden but paradoxically a poem about the poet's psychological bond with the country of his birth which he has left behind. He laments the fact that he has been far away from the country; the note of keen nostalgia breaks through in the following lines:

In that enchanted land of moon? My heart faints
And my tongue falters: For long ago, Myvanwy,
Deep in the east where now but evening gathers,
Lost is my country. (42)

The last stanza is more a stanza about his love of the country and his lament over his desertion of the country than about anything else:

Lost is that country, and all but forgotten
Mid these chill breezes, yet still, oh, believe me
All her meridian suns and ardent summers
Burn in my bosom. (42)

In the poem, "Home-Thoughts," the subject is Ghose's yearning for his own country:

While I recall you o'er deep parting seas,
Lonelier have grown these cliffs, this English grass. (47)

The poet becomes obsessed with the memory of his country, and he muses on the time past when he was there:

Unsatisfied with these dead memories,
I muse, and mould from each sweet day that was
An image of the future. (47)

The poet laments that though his heart goes out to return to the country of his origin, the return does not take place physically:

> My soul may travel to you, but the sea
> Sternly puts back the pilgrim feet of life
> . . . our hearts are made to yearn.[8]

This yearning for the motherland is definitely the initial stage of the poet's nationalism and patriotism which blossom forth in his later poetry where he takes up Indian myths and legends for treatment.

Manmohan Ghose's brother, Aurobindo Ghose was a freedom fighter and a great Yogi of India. Though he became prominent in both the roles only in the twentieth century, Sri Aurobindo expressed his profound love of his country and respect for her glorious past in his poetry written during the nineteenth century.

In the poem entitled "Bankin Chandra Chatterjee," Sri Aurobindo displays his sincere love of Bengal where he was born:

> O plains, O hills, O rivers of sweet Bengal,
> O land of love and flowers, the spring-bird's call
> And southern wind are sweet among your trees:
> Your poet's words are sweeter far than these.[8]

The poet's admiration for the beautiful natural scenery of Bengal and the repetition of the adjective "sweet" in connection with Bengal betoken the poet's profound love of his country. He again speaks of "the beauty and divinity" of Bengal in the same poem.

While paying tribute to Michael Madhusudan Dutt in the poem, "Madhusudan Dutt," Sri Aurobindo describes Bengali speech as "divine":

> Poet, who first with skill inspired did teach
> Greatness to our divine Bengali speech. (27)

Sri Aurobindo wrote a narrative poem entitled, "Baji Prabhou," where he treated the theme of "the historical incident of the heroic self-sacrifice of Baji Prabhou Deshpande, who to cover Shivaji's retreat, held the pass of Rangana for two hours with a small company of men against twelve thousand Moguls." (279) As he deals with the heroism and self-sacrifice of Baji Prabhou, he often gives vent to patriotic sentiments. For example, Baji is urged to save the nation's destiny:

But more today,
O Baji, save than any single life,—
Thy nation's destiny. (282)

Baji, on whom falls the difficult responsibility of saving the nation's destiny, shows iron will, firm determination and absolute self-confidence, and inspires the same in the select band of his handful followers:

He [Baji] gazed and cried: "Make iron of your souls
Yet if Bhavani wills, strength and the sword
Can stay our nation's future from o'erthrow
Till victory with Shivaji return." (289)

Though Baji ultimately succumbs, he does it heroically. Tanaji Malasure pays tribute to Baji:

"thirty and three the gates
By which thou enterest heaven, thou fortunate soul,
Thou valiant heart. So when my hour arrives,
May I too clasp my death, saving the land." (293)

Even though Sri Aurobindo's poetic output during the nineteenth century is meagre, his nationalism and patriotism are quite manifest throughout his work of this period.

Though Vivekananda has written several prose essays and books on India, and the duties and devotion of Indians to their motherland, he has not written many poems on the subject. However, his poems are imbued with his patriotic zeal and enthusiasm.

His love of the country is manifest in his love of Indian spirituality that he propagated to the outside world. The clarion call is given in his poem entitled "To the Awakened India." The poem begins with the clarion call:

Once more awake! . . .
Resume thy march
. . . yet strong and steady,
Blissful, bold, and free. Awakener, ever
Forward![9]

Vivekananda's nationalism and patriotism are revealed through his persuasion of his countrymen to follow the path of spiritual enlightenment.

In conclusion, it may be observed that the nationalism and patriotism that swayed the hearts of the Bengalis during the Renaissance period found varied expression in the English poetry written by the Bengalis during the nineteenth century. This poetry records their nationalism and patriotism while embodying their recapitulation of the glorious past of India, their love of the scenic beauty of Bengal, their desire to urge on Indians to build a new India and realize the spiritual greatness of Indian philosophy of life.

NOTES

1. K.R. Srinivasa Iyengar, "Indian Writing in English," *Contemporary Indian Literature* (New Delhi, 1957), p. 35.
2. R.K. Dasgupta, Foreword, *Poems of Henry Louis Vivian Derozio* (Calcutta, 1980), p. C.
3. John B. Alphonoso-Karkala, *Indo-English Literature in the Nineteenth Century* (Mysore, 1970), p. 38.
4. M.K. Naik, *A History of Indian English Literature* (New Delhi, 1978), p. 23.
5. V.K. Gokak, ed., *The Golden Treasury of Indo-Anglian Poetry* (New Delhi, 1978), pp. 6-7.
6. Toru Dutt, *Ancient Ballads and Legends of Hindustan*, ed. A.N. Dwivedi (Bareilly, 1976), p. 181.
7. Manmohan Ghose, *Collected Poems* (Calcutta, 1970), Vol. I, p. 41.
8. Sri Aurobindo, *Collected Poems* (Pondicherry, 1972), p. 25.
9. Swami Vivekananda, *The Complete Works* (Calcutta, 1978), Vol. IV, p. 387.

Summing Up

The nineteenth-century English poetry of Bengal is a literary phenomenon that cannot be brushed aside as an eccentric literary endeavour. It grew out of a cross-section of historical events taking place one after another as well as simultaneously in the nineteenth-century Bengal.

There was, however, an element of the unforeseen in the shaping of this peculiar literary product. Nobody could presuppose that an alien tongue like English would reach Bengal from such a far-away place, and capture the heart and imagination of the Bengalis with such irresistible compulsion in the course of a century or so. However, before the imaginative handling of English could be accomplished by the Bengalis, English acquired a high social status among the Bengalis as it was the language of the ruler. At the same time, English became very dear to the Bengalis as it opened for them the road to international enlightenment out of the parochial superstitious gloom that hung over Bengal for the preceding three centuries.

Thus, the choice of English as a medium of poetic expression by the Bengalis during the years of the Bengal Renaissance was emotionally a complex one. Multiple emotional urges forced the Bengalis to choose English as the medium. The choice was a forced one; at the same time, it was a spontaneous one. If the past events of those days are marshalled out now, it will be found logical to conclude that the Bengal Renaissance was never complete without the phenomenon of the nineteenth-century English poetry of Bengal.

While considering the historical facts, we, as critics of literary history, cannot ignore the emotional impact that those facts made upon the sensitive and imaginative poets who chronicled the history of the time. Hence we may conclude that the event of the appearance of the Englishman in Bengal and the domination of the Englishman and his language over Bengal were succeeded not only by a series of events of upheaval in the province but also by the emergence of the new literary phenomenon called "English poetry by Bengalis".

Once, however, the choice of the medium was decided upon, the Bengali poets writing in English found their inspirational stimulus in the events occurring in the social and political set-up of the place. From

Derozio to Sri Aurobindo, the source of inspiration had remained the same: the sorrowful spectacle of the social and political bondage of India in contrast to the pure and pristine independent and vigorous, cultural glory of ancient India. Thus we find that both the choice of the medium and the selection of the material in the nineteenth-century English poetry of Bengal were closely related to the social and political scene of Bengal of that time.

The nineteenth-century English poetry of Bengal indeed has a close social relevance. It mirrors the contemporary social scene graphically. All the major characteristics of the Bengal Renaissance are reflected in this poetry. On the one hand, the Bengal Renaissance gave rise to the growth of the nineteenth-century English poetry of Bengal. On the other hand, the nineteenth-century English poetry of Bengal embodied all the salient features of the Renaissance movement.

Apart from its social and historical relevance, the nineteenth-century English poetry of Bengal is also remarkable for its embodiment of the glorification of man, which is a characteristic of the Renaissance in Europe. The idea of independence of man, the expansion of the frontiers of human knowledge, the estimation of the richness of human culture, and the evaluation of love in human relationship are all expressed in this poetry; and, on this account, it can claim a universality of appeal and significance.

Thus, though the origin and growth of English poetry of Bengal might have been a local phenomenon, its significance has crossed the limits of the locality. Though the phenomenon is imitative in external expression, the source of its inspiration has been a genuine one. The vitality of this poetry may be measured and appreciated better when one considers the continuance and development of this poetry in the next century even after the British who introduced English had left the subcontinent.

The true end of poetry is always human. The aim of the nineteenth-century English poetry of Bengal was to reflect the human situation prevailing in Bengal at that time. The humanity of this poetry accounts for its survival over the passage of time. The merit and position of this poetry cannot be challenged. Without this poetry, where would have been the twentieth-century Indian English poetry? Even if the nineteenth-cenury English poetry of Bengal cannot claim to be great poetry, it certainly has done its job of building up a pedestal foundation and a springboard for the future English poetry of India. If we look up the initial history of the poetry of any other Commonwealth country, we will find an identical situation and background leading to the growth of a new and vital poetry.

Bibliography

Primary Sources

Anthologies

Dunn, T.O.D., ed. *The Bengali Book of English Verse*. Bombay, 1918.

Dwivedi, A.N., ed. *Indian Poetry in English*. New Delhi, 1980.

Gokak, V.K., ed. *The Golden Treasury of Indo-Anglian Poetry*. New Delhi, 1978.

Lahiri, K.C., ed. *Indo-English Poetry in Bengal*. Calcutta, 1974.

Palgrave, F.T., ed. *The Golden Treasury*. London, 1963.

Peacock, W., ed. *English Verse*. Vols. II-V. London, 1966.

The Dutt Family Album. London, 1870.

Individual Works:
(a) Bengali Poets

Derozio, H.L.V. *The Fakeer of Jungheera*. Calcutta, 1828.

_____. *Poems*. London, 1923; rpt., Calcutta, 1980.

Dutt, Gooroo Churn. *School Hours*. Calcutta, 1839.

Dutt, Greece Chunder. *Cherry Bloosom*. London, 1887.

Dutt, Hur Chunder. *Fugitive Pieces*. Calcutta, 1851.

_____. *Lotus Leaves*. Calcutta, 1871.

Dutt, Ishan Chunder. *Essays and Poems*, Calcutta, 1872.

Dutt, Michael Madhusudan. *Visions of the Past*. 1848.

_____. *The Captive Ladie*. 1949.

_____. *Madhusudan Rachnavali*, ed. Khetra Gupta. Calcutta, 1982.

Dutt, Rajnarain. *Osmyn: An Arabian Tale*. Calcutta, 1841.

Dutt, Soshee Chunder. *Miscellaneous Poems*. Calcutta, 1848.

_____. *Stray Leaves*. Calcutta, 1864.

_____. *A Vision of Sumeru and Other Poems*, Calcutta, 1878.

Dutt, Toru. *Ancient Ballads and Legends of Hindustan*. London, 1885; rpt. Bareilly, 1976.

Ghose, Aurobindo. *Songs to Myrtilla*. Calcutta, 1895.

_____. *Urvasie*. 1896.

_____. *Collected Poems*. Pondicherry, 1972.

Ghose, Kasiprasad. *The Shair or Minstrel and Other Poems*. Calcutta, 1830.

Ghose, Manmohan. *Love Songs and Elegies*. London, 1898.

_____. *Songs of Love and Death*. London, 1926.

_____. *Collected Poems*, Vol. I. Calcutta, 1970.

Ghose, Nobo Kissen. *Poetical Works*. Calcutta, 1919.

Roy, D.L. *The Lyrics of Ind*. London, 1886.

Tagore, Jotindra Mohan. *Flights of Fancy*. Calcutta, 1881.

Swami Vivekananda. *The Complete Works*. Vol. IV. Calcutta, 1978.

(b) British Poets

Byron, Lord. *The Poetical Works*. London, 1970.

Keats, John. *The Poetical Works*. London, 1959.

Milton, John. *The Poetical Works*. London, 1958.

Scott, Walter. *The Poetical Works*. London, 1971.

Shelley, P.B. *The Poetical Works*. London, 1960.

Tennyson, Alfred. *The Poems and Plays*. New York, 1938.

Wordsworth, William. *The Poetical Works*. London, 1959.

Secondary Sources

Alphonso-Karkala, John B. *Indo-English Literature in the Nineteenth-Century*. Mysore, 1970.

Bagal, Jogesh Chandra. *Derozio* (In Bengali). Calcutta, 1976.

Basu, Lotika. *Indian Writers of English Verse*. Calcutta, 1933.

Bose, Amalendu. *Michael Madhusudan Dutt*. New Delhi, 1981.

Bose, Nemai Sadhan. *Indian Awakening and Bengal*. Calcutta, 1976.

Das, Harihar. *Life and Letters of Toru Dutt*. London, 1921.

Das, Manoj. *Sri Aurobindo*. New Delhi, 1982.

Dasgupta, R.K. Introduction, *Poems of H.L.V. Derozio*. Calcutta, 1980.

Edwards, Thomas. *Henry Derozio*. Calcutta, 1884.

Ghose, Lotika. *Manmohan Ghose*. New Delhi, 1975.

Ghosh, Benoy. *Bidrohi Derozio* (In Bengali). Calcutta, 1961.

Gokak, V.K. *English in India: Its Present and Future*. Bombay, 1964.

Gupta, Atul Chandra, ed. *Studies in the Bengal Renaissance*. Calcutta, 1958.

King, Bruce, ed. *Literature of the World in English*. London, 1974.

Kokoty, P.C. *Indo-English Poetry*. Gauhati, 1969.

Macaulay, T.B. *Prose and Poems*. Cambridge, Mass., 1952.

Madge, E.W. *Henry Derozio the Eurasian Poet and Reformer*. Calcutta, 1967.

Majumdar, B.B. *History of Political Thought from Rammohan to Dayanand*. Calcutta, 1934.

Majumdar, R.C. *Glimpses of Bengal in the Nineteenth-Century*. Calcutta, 1960.

______. *History of the Freedom Movement of India*, Vol. I. Calcutta, 1971.

_____. *Renascent India*. Calcutta, 1976.

McCutchion, David. *Indian Writing in English*. Calcutta, 1968.

Munshi, K.M. *Rabindranath and Indian Renaissance*. Santiniketan, 1961.

Naik, M.K. *A History of Indian English Literature*. New Delhi, 1982.

_____, et al, ed. *Critical Essays on Indian Writing in English*. Dharwar, 1968.

_____, ed. *Indian Response to English Poetry*. Madras, 1970.

Narasimhaiah, C.D. *The Swan and the Eagle*. Mysore, 1969.

Nehru, Jawaharlal. *The Discovery of India*. Bombay, 1961.

Oaten, E.F. *A Sketch of Anglo-Indian Literature*. London, 1908.

Pal, B.C. *Memoirs of My Life and Times*, Vol. II. Calcutta, 1973.

Roy, Raja Rammohan. *The English Works*. Allahabad, 1906.

Sampson, George. *The Concise Cambridge History of English Literature*. Cambridge, 1941.

Sarkar, J.N. *History of Bengal*. Dacca.

_____. *India through the Ages*. Calcutta, 1962.

Sarkar, Susobhan. *On the Bengal Renaissance*. Calcutta, 1979.

Sengupta, Padmini. *Toru Dutt*. New Delhi, 1977.

Sengupta, Pallav. *Kavi Derozio* (In Bengali). Calcutta, 1980.

Sharp, Henry. *Selections from Educational Records*, Vol. I. Calcutta, 1920.

Spear, Percival. *The Oxford History of Modern India*. New Delhi, 1978.

Srinivasa Iyengar, K.R. *Indian Writing in English*. New Delhi, 1983.

_____. *The Indian Contribution to English Literature*. Bombay, 1945.

Tagore, Saumyendranath. *Raja Rammohan Roy*. New Delhi, 1977.

Verghese, C. Paul. *Problems of the Indian Creative Writer in English*. Bombay, 1971.

Walsh, William. *Commonwealth Literature*. London, 1973.

Williams, H.M. *Indo-Anglian Literature*. Madras, 1976.

Index